WHERE
HAVE
ALL THE
CHURCH MEMBERS
GONE?

WHERE
HAVE
ALL THE
CHURCH MEMBERS
GONE?

How to Avoid
the Five Traps That
Silently Kill Churches

A LEADERSHIP FABLE

THOM S. RAINER

CHURCH ANSWERS RESOURCES

Visit Tyndale online at tyndale.com.

Visit Tyndale Momentum online at tyndalemomentum.com.

Tyndale, Tyndale's quill logo, *Tyndale Momentum*, and the Tyndale Momentum logo are registered trademarks of Tyndale House Ministries. Tyndale Momentum is a nonfiction imprint of Tyndale House Publishers, Carol Stream, Illinois.

Where Have All the Church Members Gone?: How to Avoid the Five Traps That Silently Kill Churches

Designed by Mark Anthony Lane II

The author is represented by Alive Literary Agency, www.aliveliterary.com.

Scripture quotations are taken from the *Holy Bible*, New Living Translation, copyright © 1996, 2004, 2015 by Tyndale House Foundation. Used by permission of Tyndale House Publishers, Carol Stream, Illinois 60188. All rights reserved.

The URLs in this book were verified prior to publication. The publisher is not responsible for content in the links, links that have expired, or websites that have changed ownership after that time.

For information about special discounts for bulk purchases, please contact Tyndale House Publishers at csresponse@tyndale.com, or call 1-855-277-9400.

Library of Congress Cataloging-in-Publication Data

A catalog record for this book is available from the Library of Congress.

ISBN 978-1-4964-4875-0

Printed in the United States of America

30	29	28	27	26	25	24
7	6	5	4	3	2	1

To Maggie Rainer,
my first granddaughter.
Total joy, total love.

And always to Nellie Jo.
Your children stand up and bless you.
Your grandchildren acclaim you with joy.
Your husband marvels at such a gift of grace.

Contents

Foreword by Carey Nieuwhof *ix*

Introduction *1*

1 A Nagging Uncertainty *5*

2 Has Anyone Seen Jill? *13*

3 What Do We Really Believe? *27*

4 The Low Bar of Expectations *43*

5 That Membership Thing *57*

6 The Uprising *71*

7 The No-Go Church *87*

8 Sorting It All Out *101*

9 Where Does Your Church Go from Here? *117*

About the Author *133*

Foreword

IF YOU'RE A PASTOR, you know that somehow everything has changed over the past few years. But you may not be quite sure *how* or *why* things have changed.

Where Have All the Church Members Gone? will help you put your finger on why people aren't attending church as often as they once did. Even more important, it will give you a blueprint for moving forward.

I recognized many of the trends that Thom Rainer outlines in this book. Though I work with a lot of American leaders, I grew up and live in Canada. So many characteristics of the post-Christian culture that defined my childhood and ministry are now typical of life in the US as well, even life in the Bible Belt.

Thom Rainer does a brilliant job of showing how those trends have taken hold in day-to-day small-town, small-church life—declining attendance, drifting beliefs, lesser involvement, and the devaluing of church attendance by many who used to attend regularly.

Those developments can all seem puzzling until you understand what's really going on. This book will help make clear what currently seems mysterious.

If you've been in ministry for a while, Thom will show you how to move forward to create a *new* church in an existing church that may have become a little too stuck in the past. If you're a seasoned pastor, like Oliver, the main character in the fable, this book will give you a fresh vision for the years remaining in your ministry.

It's a whole new world, and I'm grateful that you and I get to lead in it. Thom Rainer is a valuable guide in the midst of it all.

CAREY NIEUWHOF
Author of *At Your Best*
and host of the *Carey
Nieuwhof Leadership
Podcast*

Introduction

I HAVE CONSULTED WITH CHURCHES and worked with church leaders since 1988. Do you know what that means? First, it means I'm old. But it also means I have a lot of experience, having worked with thousands of churches and pastors.

Over the past several decades, I have noticed an emerging pattern of challenges and problems in churches, particularly in North America. Each church has its own distinct context and characteristics, but they have many things in common as well. With unhealthy churches in particular, I began to see several common traps they had fallen into—traps that were silently killing them.

I continue to be amazed at how widespread these traps have become. It's not unusual to work with churches that have all five. Many more churches have three or four.

I'm also amazed by how few church leaders truly recognize the dysfunction in their churches. To be fair, these leaders are smart and caring and discerning. But for a number of reasons, they are blind to the problems that are undermining their ministries. Often, their only context is their own church in their own community, and they typically don't have points of reference to compare their challenges to those of other churches—especially if they have been at the same church for a long time. There's something to be said for getting a fresh outside perspective from time to time.

When COVID-19 hit, we saw an acceleration and exacerbation of the negative trends in many churches. Before COVID, our Church Answers team received about one request a week for a consultation. Since the pandemic, it's not unusual to get three or four requests in a week. The small cracks in the ministry foundation of many churches were not so noticeable until they suddenly became major fissures from an earthquake of cultural changes. Most of our consultation requests now don't begin with "Are we healthy?" They begin with "What happened to us?!"

This book looks at five traps that can silently kill a church. Though by no means an exhaustive list, these five traps are some of the most common found in struggling churches.

It's fair to ask how many churches are struggling today. The answer is an ambiguous "many," depending on how you define *church health*. Using the metrics described in this book, I would say that as many as 85 percent of American churches are unhealthy to a significant degree.

While that may sound like a dire proclamation, the situation is not hopeless by any means. As the body of Christ, the church has the power of God behind us and the hope we find in Jesus Christ.

The title we've chosen, *Where Have All the Church Members Gone?*, might suggest that a numerical measure of membership and attendance provides an accurate gauge of church health. In reality, the problems are much deeper than a superficial measure of attendance. Nevertheless, declining attendance can be, and usually is, a symptom of deeper problems.

That is where our story begins—in a fictional but true-to-life church in Rolesville, North Carolina, a real town in a beautiful location not far from Raleigh. My hope and prayer is that you will be able to immerse yourself in the story and relate to each of the characters. By using an allegory, I hope to awaken you to possible problems and challenges in your own church.

One thing is certain: You cannot begin to change until you understand and acknowledge that you *need* to change.

In the last chapter, I will recap and discuss the five traps in detail—from a nonfictional perspective—and I will point you and your church toward possible solutions. Indeed, my team and I will provide updated solutions regularly at our website: WhereHaveAllTheChurchMembersGone.com.

The local church is not a typical organization; it is built on the foundation of Christ's work, and it continues through the power of the Holy Spirit. I hope you will hear clearly that *every* church must depend on the power of God, and we must diligently pursue God's will through the power of prayer.

Speaking of prayer, I began praying for you before this book was even published. I have prayed for the church you represent. I have prayed that this book will point you to confront with courage the challenges your church faces. But mostly I have prayed that you will see that no challenge is insurmountable in the power of Christ.

Now it's time to introduce you to Pastor Oliver Wagner, the well-intentioned pastor of Connection Church. I hope you'll like him. I'm almost certain you will identify with him.

It is time to answer the question "Where have all the church members gone?"

1

A NAGGING UNCERTAINTY

OLIVER WAGNER LEANED BACK in his padded office chair and took a deep breath—but it came out as more of a sigh. Though he'd been a pastor for more than three decades, he had never before felt such uncertainty and apprehension. A month earlier, he had notched his eighth year as lead pastor of Connection Church, and at age fifty-nine, he sincerely hoped this church would be his last. He loved the people, loved the community, and he and Melanie were happy there. Their three grown sons were all married now and doing well—and the five grandchildren, with number six on the way, were a total joy. The empty-nest phase had turned out to be not all that empty because he and Melanie had become on-call babysitters for the grandkids—and loved it.

The church had a good reputation in the community of Rolesville, North Carolina, a town of about ten thousand not far from Raleigh. When Oliver first arrived at the church, the area was already in the midst of significant transition, growing from a small agricultural community into a rapidly expanding suburban town. At first, most of the members of Connection Church were the old guard of the community; but the past eight years had brought a healthy number of new members— people new to the area, many drawn by Rolesville's proximity to Research Triangle Park. Oliver considered the blend of old and new at the church a blessing.

And yet, something wasn't quite right. Oliver sensed it more than knew it, and he wished he could put his finger on the exact cause.

To be sure, there had been some challenges along the way. The first few years had been the toughest as he led the church through a name change—from Hanson Memorial Church, after a major donor to the church's first building campaign more than eighty years ago, to the current Connection Church—and Oliver had tried unsuccessfully to start a new members class. That one still bothered him, because he'd never understood the resistance that arose from some of the congregation's old guard. But being a conflict avoider by nature, he hadn't pushed it, and things had eventually settled down. The church seemed to be doing fine now, and the conflicts were comparatively few— certainly nothing out of the ordinary.

So why am I so uneasy?

When he had first started feeling this way, he thought maybe God was calling him to another church. But after several long and prayerful conversations with Melanie, they both concluded that they were to stay at Connection Church. They were willing to move if they sensed God's will in it, but they hadn't discerned any prompting in that direction.

Oliver pushed his thoughts aside and reached for his Bible. He always tried to anchor his mornings with an hour of prayer and Scripture reading before moving on to the demands of the day—and though he wasn't always successful, and often felt guilty for his lack of consistency, today had started off well. He took encouragement from the Gospel of Matthew and prayed for several concerns that had come up during the week. But soon his mind began to wander back to other thoughts and distractions.

What is wrong with me? Why am I unable to concentrate? And why do I feel so unsettled about the church when everything seems to be in good order? At least on the surface . . .

With a sudden burst of energy, Oliver set his Bible aside, cleared some room on his desk by stacking the books he had gathered to help with sermon preparation, and pulled out a fresh yellow legal pad and his favorite pen. With no particular plan other than to brainstorm, he began jotting some notes as things came to mind about the church.

Drawing a line down the middle of the page, he wrote "400+ Members" on one side and "~200 Weekly Attendance" on the other. He had never been much of a numbers guy, not wanting to get caught up in the attendance trap, counting nickels and noses as signs of success. But still, the gap between membership and attendance was eye-opening. COVID-19 had certainly had an effect on church attendance, and like a lot of churches, Connection Church had been slow to bounce back after the pandemic. But that was several years ago now, and Oliver knew they couldn't keep blaming things on COVID. There had to be more to it than that.

On the left-hand side of the page, he added the word "Ministries," with a corresponding "Trouble Finding Volunteers" on the right.

Though the church still kept a full slate of ministries and activities, it was tougher than ever to find enough willing volunteers.

But that's the nature of the world today, he reasoned. *Every family is so incredibly busy.*

There were several dozen young families in the church, and they were among the busiest. And even when people did volunteer, they didn't always follow through as expected. In fact, just last week, one of the preschool Sunday school leaders told Oliver that three people had failed to show up for their time slots. No notification. No apologies. They just didn't come.

And then there was *giving*—again, not something he wanted to focus on too much, as long as the bills were getting paid. Which they were. But while the tithe had held pretty steady during the pandemic—maybe because people weren't spending as much on other things—there had been a noticeable decline in the offering over the past eighteen months.

People just don't seem as enthusiastic about, or committed to, the church as they once did, he mused. *But of course a pastor's going to say that, right? Maybe I should get a second opinion.*

He retrieved his phone from under a stack of papers on his desk and scrolled through his contacts until he found the number for Jorge Miranda, perhaps the most key influencer in the church. Jorge was a long-serving elder, well-respected in the congregation, and though the elders rotated the chairman's role, he was the de facto leader even when he wasn't in charge. Connection Church was largely congregational in polity, but the elders still had significant influence. Jorge had a very successful business in the community and was often in demand for speaking engagements and to counsel other business leaders. He was known as a straight shooter, and Oliver felt confident in going to him for help.

"Hey, Pastor," Jorge said when he picked up the phone. "What can I do for you?"

"I was hoping I could stop by and talk to you this afternoon," Oliver replied. "There's something I want to run by you."

"Okay, I have some time today. Tell you what: I'll swing by the church around two."

≡

"Thanks for taking the time, Jorge," Oliver began as the two men settled into the overstuffed armchairs in the pastor's office. "With all the responsibilities you have, I try not to bother you, but I needed an ear and maybe some advice."

Jorge smiled and nodded. "I always have time for you, Oliver, and I'm always happy to help. What's on your mind?"

"My problem," Oliver said, "is one that that I don't quite know how to articulate. I just have a sense that something's not right. I'm really restless and finding myself distracted. And I think it has to do with how things are going with the church. It feels like people are coming, but their hearts aren't in it—at least not the way they used to be."

"I agree," Jorge interjected.

Oliver was surprised by Jorge's quick response. He had planned to offer further clarification, and he was a bit taken aback by the abruptness of Jorge's agreement.

"Look, Oliver, I sense it too. I've been at the church a long time, through good times and bad. But we are in a period now that is unlike any other I can recall. I want to say it's apathy, but that doesn't quite explain it. But something is definitely not right."

Oliver liked the fact that he wasn't alone in his uneasiness. *At least I'm not going crazy!* But he wasn't sure how comfortable he was knowing that the most influential person in the congregation felt that something was wrong with the church.

"I think the fact that we're both feeling the same way means that God is trying to get our attention," Jorge continued. "We need to act on it."

Oliver was not surprised by Jorge's call to action. The business leader was nothing if not decisive, even if he didn't have an immediate answer.

"I just wish I had a better understanding of how to lead this church into the future," Oliver said. "I mean, this is still the Bible Belt, but it feels as if everything else in the culture is shifting around us."

"Well, Pastor," Jorge said with a slight twinkle in his eye, "I don't think God intends for you to figure it out all on your own. If you want my advice, I suggest we assemble a small team from a cross section of the congregation—maybe six or eight people, to keep it manageable—to discuss and pray about the direction of the church. I'm confident that God will show us the reasons for our discomfort and will lead us in the way we should go."

Oliver immediately warmed to the idea. "I've been thinking about creating a long-term planning committee to look at the church's next ten years," he said. "By then, I'll likely be ready to pass the baton of pastoral leadership and guide the church through a fruitful transition to a new pastor."

"Honestly, I was thinking of something more focused and short-term," Jorge replied. "Like a task force. I've always believed that churches should have very few ongoing committees— usually just finance and personnel. As soon as you put the words *long-term* and *committee* together, you risk ending up with a group that will last beyond its usefulness and become just another meeting for meeting's sake."

"I think we can agree that we don't need another one of those," Oliver said with a laugh.

"I also don't think we need to connect that plan directly with your own future," Jorge continued. "Our current focus should be on finding an answer to the uneasiness we're both feeling. What say we get a date on the calendar, and let's each invite two or three stakeholders from the congregation to join the group."

Ever the optimist, Oliver was quick to agree. But he could not have imagined where this idea would lead. If he had known, he might have stopped everything and learned to live with his restlessness and the status quo.

Yes, there would be some exceedingly difficult days ahead.

2

HAS ANYONE SEEN JILL?

AS OLIVER DROVE TO THE CHURCH on the evening set for the meeting of the first Vision Task Force, as they had decided to call it, he felt a palpable sense of excitement. But when he walked into the conference room and saw Ken Cassidy, his most vocal critic in the congregation, seated at the table, his heart sank.

I know Jorge said we should invite a cross section of the congregation, but why did one of them have to be Ken?

He decided not to dwell on the issue. There was too much work to be done. Maybe his perpetual nemesis would give him a break and offer only constructive input. But Oliver wasn't holding out much hope. He looked around the room at the familiar faces of people he had known since coming to the church as pastor eight years ago.

In addition to Jorge, there was Rob Beecher, one of the church's longest-serving deacons, who was also an assistant principal at the high school. He was often quiet, preferring to listen rather than speak, but he had a way with people—especially with high schoolers—that had earned him a lot of respect in the community.

Next to Rob at the table was Emma Rockwell, who was chief operating officer of a large employer near Rolesville. She and her husband had joined Connection Church a few months before Oliver's arrival, even though the church had no pastor at the time. She was precise, punctual, and detailed, and her "get it done" attitude had proved to be a real asset during the name-change process. Oliver had no question about her commitment to the church.

Across from Emma was Becky Garner, whom Oliver often referred to as "the one who keeps this place together." She was running the children's program when the Wagners first arrived, but when Oliver saw her gifts in administration and leadership, he quickly moved her to the role of administrative director. Though Becky was not as strategic and proactive as either Jorge or Emma, once she was assigned a task, she would complete it with excellence—often well before it was due. She was fiercely loyal to Oliver, but she wouldn't hesitate to push back if she felt he was leading in a wrong direction.

And then there was Ken Cassidy. Again Oliver wondered why Jorge had asked Ken to serve on the task force. He had been forced into early retirement when the company where he served as a middle manager shut down. Oliver honestly didn't know how Ken had lasted there as long as he did. He was consistently argumentative, and you could count on him to present a contrary view to almost anything that had to do with change. He had led the charge against changing the name of the church and was instrumental in torpedoing the proposed new members class. Oliver decided that Jorge must know what he was doing in choosing Ken, and he vowed to show the curmudgeon as much love and respect as he could.

≡

Oliver took his seat at the head of the table and opened the meeting with prayer. He was looking forward to hearing from the other members of the task force.

This meeting could actually be fun, he said to himself. *We'll be looking forward to the days and years ahead.* He was excited about finding ways in which Connection Church could live up to its name and truly connect with people inside and outside the church.

"Based on our conversations leading up to tonight," he began, "I think we all have a general idea of what we're seeking to accomplish with this task force. The purpose of this first meeting is to 'define reality.'" He punctuated his statement with air quotes, drawing laughter from two or three people at the table. "Jorge suggested that we need to know where the church currently is before we can begin to talk about the future. So I've asked Emma to bring us up to date with an overview of where the church has been over the past five years.

"Thank you, Pastor," Emma said as she tapped a few keys on her laptop and projected a report onto the whiteboard across the room. "I know you're not a big fan of putting numbers at the forefront, but statistics are not inherently bad. Like road signs, they can point us in the right direction."

Oliver realized he was looking forward to this part of the discussion. He knew that several families had joined the church in the past few years, and he didn't think many people had left.

"As you can see," Emma continued, "there are some encouraging numbers here. For example, in the past five years, twenty-eight family units have joined the church. Those units represent nine singles and nineteen families of two or more people, bringing the total number of new members to seventy-two."

The members of the task force smiled and nodded affirmatively. Indeed, there seemed to be a lot of new faces in the church, and Emma's numbers confirmed that perception.

"During that same period," Emma said, "seven families have left the church. So if you add up everyone who has died, left for another church in the community, or moved out of the area, the total is forty-four members. To put it another way, we've added seventy-two people and lost forty-four, for a net gain of twenty-eight members in five years."

Oliver loved hearing the buzz in the room. There was a sense of joy about the accomplishments of the past, and they were ready to move on to the future.

Oliver noticed that Jorge was frowning, as if the math wasn't adding up for him. But before Oliver could think about it any further, Emma dropped the other shoe.

"But—" she said soberly.

That simple, three-letter conjunction seemed to hang in the air, and all eyes were again on Emma. Oliver could sense the mood shifting. Only Emma knew what she was about to say, but her demeanor and body language spoke volumes. The next sentence was not going to be encouraging.

"But," she repeated, "during that same five-year period, our attendance has declined by almost 20 percent. And most of that decline has taken place in the past three years."

The faces at the table were a combination of confusion and disappointment.

Emma anticipated the question that was on everyone's mind: "How can that *be*, right? We're seeing new faces almost every month. The new people in the church far outnumber those who are no longer here."

"Wait a minute!" Ken exclaimed. "If we're gaining new members in the church every year, how can attendance be down? Something doesn't smell right."

Oliver sighed. Leave it to Ken to suggest that something nefarious was happening.

"You know," Ken concluded, "we have over two hundred people attending every week, and people moving all over the building. It's hard to count *everyone*. I bet we've been missing a lot of people—maybe the kids."

A couple of nodding heads reflected the strong desire in the room to find that the numbers were wrong. But Becky quickly countered that perspective.

"Actually," she said softly, "the numbers are spot-on. "We have two people counting each section to make certain the count is correct. I have led that team for the past two years, and accuracy is very important to me. I guess I'm kind of a statistics nerd."

The room was silent, waiting for her to continue.

"But think about it," Becky said. "If our attendance is down about 20 percent, with most of the decline happening in the past three years, it means our attendance is down about 7 percent a year. But if you look at the average decline per month, it's almost imperceptible."

"So we've been declining, but most of us couldn't see it," Rob chimed in. "I guess you tend to see who's *here*; not who's *not* here."

Oliver was astounded by the information, but even more so by the fact that he hadn't been aware of it before now.

Why hasn't Becky shared this information with me? I guess she took it to heart when I said I didn't want to get caught up in attendance figures.

He could feel his face becoming flushed. His aversion to numbers meant he hadn't seen what was really taking place. The church was in decline and he didn't even know it.

Fewer people were gathering for worship.

Fewer people were gathering to hear the preaching of God's Word.

Fewer people were gathering to enjoy the fellowship and encouragement of their fellow believers.

And yet the decline was virtually invisible.

≡

The members of the task force began asking a series of questions, trying to understand how attendance could be declining without anybody knowing. Everyone was talking at once.

Then Jorge spoke up and the room fell silent again.

"Oliver, didn't you mention that you were going to invite Jill Reed to be a part of this group?"

"I did," Oliver replied, "and I sent her an invitation. In fact, I emailed her twice, but she never responded. I guess I should have followed up again."

"I was just thinking how nice it would be if Jill were here to help us figure this thing out," Jorge continued. "She has a good combination of analytical skills and plain old common sense."

There was a lull in the conversation, and Rob decided to say what seemed to be on everyone's mind.

"As a deacon, I've gotten to know a lot of the key volunteers— and by that I mean the people you know you can call on when there's a project to do or a ministry spot to fill. Jill was definitely in that camp, but I have to admit I haven't seen her around as much as I used to. It used to be you would see her almost every time the doors were open. But in the past six months or so, I don't think I've seen her much at all."

Oliver looked around and saw others nodding in affirmation. "Does anyone know anything about Jill?" he asked.

For the next several minutes, the conversation turned to the topic of Jill's whereabouts. She was well liked by everyone, but no one seemed to know what had happened to her. As the discussion continued, two or three other names came up as well.

After a while, Oliver realized they were getting pretty far afield, and though he certainly didn't want to derail a healthy conversation, he knew the meeting would not accomplish its goals if he didn't get everyone back on track.

"Folks," he implored gently, "I appreciate the concern for Jill. I will contact her tomorrow. For now, can I ask us to get back to our agenda? We were trying to figure out how we are growing but not growing."

A few people chuckled at the pastor's choice of words. Emma, however, wasn't so sure that the discussion needed to change.

"Actually, Pastor," she said, "the two conversations are more interconnected than we first thought."

"*Oh*," Oliver responded. "How so?"

"Let's look at our concern for Jill in light of our discussion about 'growing but not growing,'" Emma continued. "First, would we consider Jill a recent *addition* to our membership or a recent *deletion*?"

Her question caught Oliver off guard. He wasn't sure exactly what she was asking.

Then Jorge spoke up. "Emma, I'm not sure that's the right question. She's not either one of those. She joined our church at least five years ago, and her name is still on the roll."

"*Exactly*," Emma said. "From a membership perspective, she's neither an addition nor a subtraction. But now, in light of our conversation, does Jill attend *more* often or *less* often?"

Oliver could almost see the light bulbs going on around the table.

"Oh, I see what you're saying," Jorge said with enthusiasm. "Our membership can grow while our attendance declines, especially if a lot of members are following Jill's pattern and attending less often."

The room grew quiet as each person considered Emma's example and Jorge's response.

When Oliver broke the silence, his voice was trembling.

"I have to say I'm a bit embarrassed. I guess I should have been more aware, but I didn't know our attendance was declining. In fact, I've told my pastor friends that we've had steady and solid growth. But this issue about Jill has really gotten to me. And there are others just like her, apparently."

"It appears that Jill is slipping away from the church, and I didn't know that either," said Jorge, trying to offer some support.

Oliver swallowed hard. The meeting had not gone the way he thought it would. The moment of celebration and vision-casting had turned into a time of sobering reality and introspection.

"Seriously," Oliver continued with more composure. "Has anyone seen Jill lately?"

≡

"Oliver," Jorge said, "Given this new information, is it okay with you if we reconsider where we go from here?"

"If you have some ideas, I'm all ears," Oliver replied.

"First, though," Jorge began, "we need to be reminded how much our pastor has done for us." He paused to make eye contact with each person before continuing. "I admit I was caught off guard hearing that our attendance is declining, and it's a problem we need to address. But I think it should also be said that the fact that Pastor Wagner convened this meeting is indicative of his love for the church. It's risky for a pastor to ask for church members to help him look to the future. It almost always means change from the way he has led our congregation up to this point. I admire him for his courage."

Oliver, meanwhile, was looking at Ken, who was fidgety and seemed uncomfortable. Oliver again wished that Ken was not part of the group, but his agitation was becoming an elephant in the room.

Jorge must have noticed as well, because he immediately said, "Ken, do you have something you want to say?"

"I sure do," Ken said sharply. "We seem to have all concluded that the church needs some major overhaul because a few people have chosen to go somewhere else. I don't get it, and I don't agree. I like our church the way it is. I believe we are wasting a lot of time and energy here."

While Ken glared at the others around the table, Becky

sought to defuse the situation. She had always felt comfortable talking to Ken, despite his often gruff demeanor, and she knew that he respected her.

"Ken," she said gently, "in one sense you're right. We shouldn't have foregone conclusions. We need to be open to new information. But we have already recognized that our church is experiencing a slight decline. We have to at least look to see where God wants us in the future."

Ken did not seem satisfied with her response, but he didn't argue. Instead, he leaned back in his chair and stared silently at the ceiling, his body language speaking louder than words.

"Jorge, I agree with what you've said," Emma interjected. "But you mentioned that we might need to reconsider our direction at this point. What did you have in mind?"

Jorge smiled. Emma was all about getting down to business. It was one of the traits that had contributed to her rapid rise in the business world. He appreciated her speaking up to get the meeting back on track.

Oliver gestured for Jorge to continue. It was time to hear what he had to say.

"The meeting kind of took a turn when we started talking about Jill and some others who seem to have left our fellowship," Jorge said. "I think we need some more information—maybe ask Jill and some other church members some questions."

"Are you talking about focus groups, or some sort of formal survey?" Emma asked. "Before we launch a new product or initiative in the business world, we like to get a lot of input."

"Maybe we could do both," Jorge said.

Oliver nodded and said, "I saw something recently about a third-party evaluation process—and Becky, I think I might have mentioned it to you—but in the meantime, Jorge, I want to hear more about what you were thinking."

Though Oliver was uncomfortable with the direction of the conversation, he also felt as if they were finally getting down to brass tacks. It was an odd mixture of anxiety and anticipation.

"I think it's time to go talk with some of our members," Jorge said with assurance. "For example, we could pick two or three folks who are still very active in the church. Then we could maybe talk to Jill and one or two others who apparently are no longer coming to church. And lastly, we could talk to two or three who are still involved but are obviously attending less often. We will tell them with all honesty that we want to listen to them to get their input about the church."

Becky offered quickly, "I already have eight possible names of people who fit those categories."

Oliver smiled. It was that kind of efficiency and knowledge of the congregation that made Becky such a valuable asset to the church. Oliver knew he had done a few things well, and promoting Becky was one of them.

"Outstanding!" Jorge responded. "Eight people may not be a comprehensive survey, but it's not a bad start. I suggest we divide our assignments so that—"

Before Jorge could finish his sentence, Ken erupted out of his seat.

"I am not about to talk to these people," he said with evident emotion. "I told you it's a total waste of time. We've never done anything like this before, and the church has been just fine!"

Ken stormed out of the room and slammed the door. The room was silent for a few seconds before Jorge gave a low whistle and said, "Oliver, I don't want to pile on, but why exactly did you ask Ken to be on the task force?"

Oliver was shocked. "*I* didn't invite him. I thought *you* did."

The two men looked at each other in amazement.

"Not that we were trying to *exclude* him . . . ," Oliver said.

Everyone laughed, and Jorge said, "As I was saying . . . Becky, Emma, Rob, and I will each talk to two of the people Becky has identified. And Oliver, not that I'm trying to exclude *you* from this part of the process, but I don't want anyone to be concerned that the pastor is asking them these types of questions. They may take it the wrong way."

"I totally agree," Oliver responded. "I can focus on finding the information about that third-party evaluation process." Far from feeling excluded, he was pleased with how the process was unfolding, and he was reminded again of Jorge's wisdom and experience.

"Okay, then," Jorge concluded, "let me draft some questions, which we can finalize by email, and let's get this done quickly. I think this will open a lot of doors for conversation, and it would be great if we could get this buttoned down before our next meeting, a month from now. Who knows? We might be surprised where this leads us as a church."

His final comment would turn out to be more prescient than he realized.

3

WHAT DO WE REALLY BELIEVE?

THE NEXT MORNING, Oliver and Melanie sat down for toast and coffee before he left for the church, as had been their week-day practice for most of their thirty-seven-year marriage. The task force meeting had gone much later than Oliver had antici-pated, and Melanie had been fast asleep when he got home. Such was the life of a pastor's wife, to which she had grown accustomed.

Oliver knew that Melanie could read him like a large-print Bible. He was still coming to grips with the results of last night's meeting, and he was certain his face betrayed the fact that it hadn't gone as he had planned.

But Melanie was wise. She always seemed to know just the

right way to approach a subject and give him the freedom to process his thoughts and express himself.

"How did the meeting go?" she asked.

"I'm not sure," Oliver replied. He was clearly subdued. Melanie buttered an English muffin and remained silent. She waited for him to talk without prompting.

After taking a deep breath, Oliver explained to her how the task force meeting had taken an unexpected turn.

"When the meeting started, I was excited. But by the time I left, I was just confused." Oliver spared no detail as he shared the events from the night before.

After finishing his explanation, Oliver refilled his coffee and sat looking out the kitchen window, lost in thought.

"So, what else is bothering you?" Melanie asked gently. She knew her husband well, and it was clear that he had not yet fully articulated his frustrations.

"Well," Oliver began with some hesitation, "I mentioned early in the meeting that I would check in with Jill Reed, after her name came up in the conversation as someone we haven't seen much of lately. But by the time the meeting was over, everyone on the task force had been assigned two people to contact, including Jill, but Jorge felt that I shouldn't get involved in the conversations with church members because they might hesitate to tell the pastor the full story."

"Wise decision," Melanie said without hesitation. "I agree with Jorge."

That wasn't exactly what Oliver wanted to hear, but he

trusted his wife's opinion and knew that she simply wanted what was best for him and for the church.

Oliver smiled and said, "Have I ever told you how much I love you?"

≡

By the time Oliver reached the church office, Becky had already tracked down the information for the church evaluation program they had discussed the night before.

"It's called the Know Your Church report, from a group called Church Answers," she said. "I sent you the link."

Oliver went over to his desk, opened his laptop, and clicked the link.[†] After perusing the website for several minutes and jotting down some notes, he went back to Becky's desk to talk it through with her.

"I think this Know Your Church thing might be the way to go," he said. "It looks like an efficient way to survey the congregation and find out what people think about how the church is doing in six key areas: worship, evangelism, fellowship, discipleship, prayer, and ministry. That would be good information for us to have, to go along with what the members of the task force will find from their one-on-one conversations."

"So this is something for the whole congregation to do?" Becky asked. "How do you want to get the word out?"

"Well, we could select people to take the survey, or open it

[†] "Know Your Church Report," Church Answers, https://churchanswers.com/solutions/tools/know -your-church.

up to everyone," Oliver explained. "But to me, the more the merrier. The cost is the same either way, and I think the more information we can gather, the more reliable the results will be for guiding what we do next."

"Sounds good to me," Becky said.

"As for how to get the word out, how about if you put together a slide to add to our Sunday morning announcements, and I will introduce the idea and explain what we're thinking. Then the next thing would be to follow up with an email to the congregation that reiterates what I will share on Sunday and gives people the link to the online survey."

"Perfect!" Becky said with enthusiasm. "We have our email list ready to go. Just give me the information you want to include and I'll take care of it."

"Awesome," Oliver replied. "I think we should give people two or three weeks to complete the survey, maybe with a reminder email after ten days or so. And then, according to the website, the report comes back pretty quickly after that, so we should have everything in time for our task force meeting next month."

Over the next few weeks, as Oliver waited for the results of the Know Your Church survey to come back, the rest of the task force reached out to the people they had agreed to contact.

≡

Emma had been chosen to meet with Jill, as one of two task force interviews with people who had stopped coming to the church after being involved for some time.

The two women met at a popular local coffee shop that had once been a pizza parlor. The quaint industrial décor was typical of many coffee places, but the seating area was much larger than at the other shops in town, allowing customers to find a private place to talk. Jill said she was happy to share her thoughts, so Emma started with the list of conversation starters that Jorge had drafted: What did Jill think of the church? Why had she become less active? What ultimately led her to drop out?

"Well, you know that I've worked in the Sunday school program," Jill began. "Which only seemed right because my three kids were going there. And that was fine, but basically you're hanging out with kids and not necessarily having a chance to interact much with the other adults in the room. And I've gone to some of the women's things, but I'm working—I manage an insurance office—so I'm not really available to attend the weekday Bible study."

"What about a small group?" Emma interjected. "Those meet in the evening, and—"

"Well, I don't know if you know this, but this is a second marriage for both my husband and me. He was raised Catholic and really isn't interested in going to church. He's fine with me taking the kids, but he's got other things to do—so he says—on Sunday mornings. And I didn't feel comfortable going to a small group on my own. I don't want to be the fifth wheel somewhere."

"So it sounds like you've gotten involved in some things, but . . ."

"Well, that's the thing. It seems like there's a lot of activities—busy, busy, busy—and that's fine, but not a lot of real connection. I feel like I was there and I was active, but nobody really noticed me beyond that."

"Wow, I'm so sorry," Emma said.

"It is what it is. No hard feelings."

≡

Jorge met with Hank and Rebecca Stevens, a couple he had known for almost two decades. During that time, they had served the church in countless roles. They had invited Jorge over to their home for the interview, and they were happy to talk about the church, but there seemed to be something unspoken just beneath the surface of their responses. Finally, Rebecca just blurted it out.

"Hank and I have decided to take a break from serving for a while," she said. "We have been doing some kind of ministry at church for our entire married life. We've done our time. It's time for someone else to step up."

Hank nodded in affirmation. Though he chose not to elaborate, his body language spoke volumes. He was done.

Jorge didn't know what to say in response to their announcement, and after a few more minutes of polite conversation, he thanked them for their time and stood to go.

"Don't worry, Jorge," Rebecca said. "We'll still be there on Sunday mornings. We just need a season to ourselves."

≡

One of Rob Beecher's interviews was with Mark and Kate O'Brien, a young couple with four kids, twelve and under. What they shared was a familiar story.

"With club sports, ballet, and music," Mark said, "the kids keep us pretty busy. As you know, a lot of sporting events are on Sunday mornings . . . and even when they're not, sometimes we're just so exhausted from a week of activities that we take a break from church on Sunday. To be honest, we missed six weeks in a row last summer with travel softball."

"Do you think you were missed at church after being gone so long?" Rob asked.

"Sure, we got some texts and some social media contacts," Kate responded. "But everyone was great about it. They understood. Many of them are in the same boat. You can't always go to church when your family is so busy."

≡

Becky met with Dean and Maria Covington, a couple in their late forties, who had not been back to weekly in-person attendance since COVID.

"I think we make too much of attending church," Maria said, using air quotes to punctuate the last two words. "The church is not a building. It's the people. It doesn't really matter where we are. We don't have to be in a church building together. In fact, we don't have to be anywhere together. We are the church wherever we are."

"We've gotten back together occasionally with our small group," Dean added. "That seems to fit our schedule better anyway . . ."

≡

After her meeting with the Covingtons, Becky called the other task force members for an informal debriefing. Then she stopped by Oliver's office.

"Hey, Becky. What's up?"

"I know you're aware that the rest of us have been having conversations with past and present members of Connection, right?"

"Yes, and I understand Jorge's reasoning for not wanting me directly involved."

"Well, even though our next meeting isn't for another three days, I was curious to know what the other task force members were hearing in their conversations. So I called Jorge, Emma, and Rob for an informal debriefing."

"Okay . . ."

"After hearing the various reports, I just decided to come to you and recap the conversations. I didn't want you to get blindsided at the meeting. I'm just afraid that some of the feedback might upset you."

Her concern was well-founded. In fact, Oliver wanted to scream. *Taking a break from church? We've done our time? It's time for someone else to step up? Can't go to church because your family is busy? The church doesn't have to be anywhere together?* These were lifelong church members and attenders saying these things. They weren't the unchurched. They weren't the "nones." In fact, some of these couples were among the most active in the congregation. Not too long ago, they would have hardly ever missed attending a Sunday worship service. Not to mention Wednesday nights.

"What is going on?" Oliver threw up his hands in amazement. "What has changed in our culture to where serving in the church is now described like a prison sentence? *Doing time?* How have we allowed travel sports and other activities to take priority over worshiping God with a gathering of other believers? How did we get to a point where attending church is option number four out of four options? It really wasn't all that long ago, Becky, that church attendance was the first option for most folks, and everything else came next. Where is the *commitment* now? Where have all the church members gone?"

And that wasn't even the worst of it. The real bombshell would land later that day in the form of the Know Your Church survey results.

≡

There was a lot to digest in the responses to the 160 questions, so at first Oliver simply skimmed through the pages, which had an assortment of answers highlighted in Green (Healthy), Yellow (Marginally Healthy), and Red (Very Unhealthy). Most of the categories seemed to be yellow, but when he reached the final category—Doctrine—his heart leapt into his throat as several questions highlighted in red jumped out at him. One in particular left him stunned and speechless.

The only way to heaven is through a personal relationship with Christ.

Strongly Agree	19.6%
Agree	32.7%
Undecided	18.0%
Disagree	16.3%
Strongly Disagree	13.4%

Oliver did a quick tally as he slumped in his chair: 47.7 percent of respondents either were undecided or outright disagreed with what Jesus said about himself in John 14:6.

How is this even possible?

How could someone be a member of Connection Church and not even affirm our basic beliefs?

How could we have failed to communicate the importance of such a fundamental truth?

Oliver was beyond flabbergasted. He loved God's Word. He believed God's Word. Somehow, though, the message was not getting through to the members of the congregation.

Before he could think any more about it, Carol, his assistant, interrupted and told him that Ken Cassidy was on the phone.

"He said to interrupt any meeting you are in," she said sheepishly. "I am so sorry."

"Could the day get any worse?" Oliver muttered under his breath. Yes, it could.

≡

"Now, Ken, just calm down a minute," Oliver said for the umpteenth time. It was conversations like this that sometimes made him question his calling as a pastor.

"But Ken, we have not even begun to think about any changes."

"No, the survey was not a ploy to get everything I want at the church."

"That is simply not true, Ken."

"No, Jorge is not controlling me."

Between each of Oliver's responses, a few minutes elapsed with Ken doing all the talking. Oliver was not able to say much at all.

Out of the corner of his eye, he saw Becky approach his office door and then turn away. Phone in hand, he got up from his chair and went after her. Becky looked back in time to see Oliver waving her back toward his office while trying to get a word in edgewise in the conversation.

"No, Ken, that is not true."

"Well, I'm sorry you feel that way."

Mercifully, the conversation soon ended. Oliver looked at the timer on his phone and saw he had spent almost a full hour listening to Ken harangue him about things he knew nothing about.

"As I'm sure you gathered," Oliver said, "that was our buddy Ken. He's convinced that the Vision Task Force is simply an underhanded approach for Jorge and me to take the church in a direction 'no one' in the church wants to go. He's ready to oppose anything the task force recommends, even though—as you know—we have no idea where we're headed."

"Ken is nothing if not passionate," Becky said, trying to lighten the mood. "So how did he end the conversation?"

"With his usual threats," Oliver said in subdued tone. "He wants the congregation to vote on everything, and he says he's going to 'gather the forces' to stop any changes."

Oliver took a sip from his water bottle before continuing.

"But truth be told, I'm much more concerned about the survey results than with anything Ken has to say." He handed Becky a printout of the results and directed her attention to the last few pages.

"In three decades of serving as a pastor, I cannot recall being this shocked about something taking place at my church."

His face was despondent, and Becky hurt to see her pastor in such pain.

"I—I don't know what to think or say," Oliver stumbled over his words. "I love the Bible. I teach the Bible. How could almost half our congregation not believe the foundational truths of Christianity?"

"Oliver," Becky said gently, "do you remember when you

named me as administrative director of the church?"

"Of course I do," Oliver replied with a small smile. "It was a great day for this church."

"Well, maybe you don't remember everything—but the current situation reminds me of it. For about two weeks, we dealt with a ton of opposition. The critics were led by you-know-who, but you were able to calm me down and give me a clear perspective."

Becky paused for a moment. "I remember those words so clearly," she said. "You told me we were going to look at each part of the problem, deal with it, and move on in God's power. And that's exactly what you did. You never had any doubt that we would prevail."

She looked at Oliver's worried face and spoke with confidence. "So now I am telling *you*. We will look at each part of the problem, deal with it, and move on in God's power."

≡

When the Vision Task Force reconvened for the follow-up meeting, everyone was anxious to hear the results of all the conversations that had taken place. As Emma, Becky, Jorge, and

> **Trap #1**
>
> Too many people in the church either do not believe the Bible or do not understand the basic truths of the Bible, because the church is not teaching the foundational truths of Scripture.

Rob gave their reports, there was evident surprise about some of the feedback.

"And that's not even the worst of it," Oliver said as he passed around printouts of the survey results along with a summary he had written of the areas most in need of attention. "But as difficult as it is to hear some of this feedback, we can be thankful for the clarity it gives us. In all my years of ministry, I've never gotten such concise and focused input on problems that must be dealt with."

Becky admired how quickly Oliver seemed to have regained his confidence. And then she found out the reason behind his rapid rebound.

"After Becky and I went over the initial survey results, I went home and talked to Melanie," Oliver said. "My wife may not have all the answers, but she always seems to point me toward some good possibilities."

"Let's hear it for Melanie," Jorge said with a grin.

"She told me we have to begin by acknowledging that we have a problem—a *big* problem. In addition to all the other input we received, almost half of those who took the Know Your Church survey told us they could not unequivocally affirm that Jesus is the only way of salvation."

Everyone at the table nodded simultaneously for Oliver to continue.

"I'm still not sure how that's possible, but Melanie and I looked at three key places where we should be teaching the truths of Scripture. The first, obviously, is that I should be

teaching them regularly in my sermons. But here's the reality—
I *don't* do that."

"That's not true," Jorge said emphatically. "You always teach
from the Bible."

"Sadly, it *is* true," Oliver responded softly. "I quickly reviewed
several of my sermons, and what I found is that I mostly preach
about *applying* biblical truths, but I rarely explicitly teach those
truths. Jorge, you get it because you already affirm our statement of beliefs deep in your heart. But I simply do not teach
the core truths sufficiently when I preach."

Oliver could see that Jorge was mulling it over. But he didn't
object further, so Oliver continued with his next point.

"The second place we should be teaching the core truths is
in our community groups." He glanced quickly at Becky to see
how she was taking this. After all, she had leadership responsibility for the community groups.

But he had no need for concern as she immediately affirmed
his observation.

"You're right, Oliver," she admitted. "Our community groups
almost all study life application books and other resources. Like
you just said about your preaching, we focus on applying the
truths without explicitly saying what those truths are."

"But we don't need to abandon application in our quest to
bring back the clear teachings of the Bible," Oliver said. "We
need balance. But for right now, we must find ways to teach
more clearly what we believe."

"So, what's the third place where we're missing it?" Emma

asked. She could always be counted on to keep the meeting moving along.

"The third would be in a new members class—which I realize we don't have right now," Oliver responded. "I think that's a topic we need to revisit as a church, notwithstanding past opposition—"

"Which is likely to happen again," Emma added. "So we need to be prepared for that."

"In a new members class," Oliver continued," everyone should be given a copy of our statement of beliefs. I mean, they're on our church website, but maybe people don't look there."

"Be that as it may," Jorge interjected, "our task is not to look back at our failures—real or imagined—but to focus on the road ahead and on what we need to do to get the church back on the right track. For now, let's be thankful that we discovered a major trap that churches can fall into, and we did it in time to address the underlying issues. So let's get to it."

As Oliver prepared to close the meeting with a word of prayer, he had a gnawing sense that they were only touching the tip of the iceberg. And indeed, the days ahead would demonstrate clearly that there was much work yet to be done.

4

THE LOW BAR
OF EXPECTATIONS

OVER THE NEXT FEW DAYS, Oliver began to come to grips with his emotions. On the one hand, he was hurt and more than a little ashamed that his leadership at the church had led to greater biblical illiteracy and maybe even lack of belief. He loved the Bible. He loved teaching the Bible. But obviously he had failed to lead the church toward a deeper understanding of it.

At the same time, he had to admit he felt a bit relieved. As painful as these latest revelations were, he valued clarity and was grateful that the problem was something he could address immediately. The issue wasn't a lack of love for the truth of Scripture; rather, it was that he hadn't been leading the church toward a greater love of God's Word.

Still, there had to be more to it. Oliver wasn't convinced that it could be that simple. As he continued muttering to himself, "There's something more," he heard a soft knock on the door.

"Come in," he said without hesitation.

When he looked up from his desk, he saw it was Becky. And she had that look on her face—the one that says, *I have an idea, and I think you're gonna like it.*

"Can we call another task force meeting as soon as possible?" she asked almost breathlessly.

Oliver laughed. "Sure, what's up?"

"Well, we've talked to a bunch of people who represent the less active and inactive members of the church. But I've been going down the membership rolls and identifying those who are *most* active."

Becky's excitement was contagious, and Oliver motioned for her to sit down in one of the overstuffed armchairs in his office.

"We've done our due diligence listening to those who don't seem committed to the church," she continued. "I figured it's time we took a look at the *committed* members to see what we can learn from *them*."

"That is a *great* idea, Becky," Oliver said. "After the past several days, it's nice to look at the positive issues in the church."

≡

Everything worked out and the task force was able to meet at five o'clock the next evening. They met in Oliver's office, and no one had asked Ken to reconsider and rejoin the group. No doubt he would have objected to the timing of the meeting, even though he was retired. Oliver felt they were better off without him.

Jorge was the last to arrive. He had stopped at a favorite deli to bring sandwiches and sodas for everyone.

That's what makes him a great leader, Oliver said to himself. *Always thinking ahead and thinking of others. A true servant's heart.*

Emma, true to form, didn't want to hear a lot of small talk. As soon as everyone was seated, she prayed for the meal. Oliver was thankful that she didn't default to the pastor, as so often happened.

"What do you have, Becky?" Emma said, again taking the initiative and getting the meeting off to a quick start. "I am dying to hear your findings!"

"I'm not sure they are *findings* as much as they are data that we need to discern as a group. I am passing out a hard copy of some information I've put together. It's a list of forty-three of the most active adults in our church."

"Interesting approach," Jorge said. "How did you define 'active' in coming up with these names?"

"It was a fairly simple process," Becky replied. "It isn't perfect, but I think it will prove helpful. I started by listing four of the most common commitments or activities that apply to church members: regular attendance at worship; being active in a community group; being involved in at least one ministry or program at the church; and some sort of involvement that reaches beyond the walls of the church—whether that's evangelism, community service, or what have you. I could have listed 'regular giving,' but I thought it would be inappropriate to discuss that kind of information with the group. Even Oliver doesn't know the level of financial giving of our members."

She paused for a moment and looked at her handout. "You will see that each of those commitments is listed at the top of the page. Then you can look horizontally for a checkmark if the person is involved in that activity."

Along with the others, Oliver looked over the pages. He liked the direction that Becky was going.

"Can you see why these particular names are on the list?" Becky asked with a smile.

Emma was the first to respond. "Each church member has at least three checkmarks. And some of them have four."

"This exercise makes perfect sense," Jorge said after swallowing a bite of his sandwich. "If we accept that these four areas are indicative of commitment by the church members, we know who our most committed people are. I totally agree that the areas you picked are excellent for measuring commitment, but I wish we were comfortable enough to add giving. That's a big indicator of faithfulness. You know what Jesus said: 'Wherever your treasure is, there the desires of your heart will also be.'"[†]

Becky smiled again. "Well," she said, "let's just say that the list wouldn't change much if we included the giving component."

Everyone seemed satisfied with her response.

Rob spoke up next. "I agree that you're on the right track here, Becky. But I wonder if we should take a few minutes to ask ourselves *why* these areas of commitment are important."

Oliver enjoyed watching the others interact, and he loved the direction the task force was taking. He didn't want to

---

[†] Matthew 6:21.

interrupt the discussion, but there was a brief pause, so he offered a suggestion.

"Can we begin with attendance at worship services? When I had to listen to Ken for almost an hour, he kept bringing up the issue of attendance. He thinks the church is too legalistic about it. I know you've heard this line from others: 'The church is the people, not the building.'"

"Yep," Emma responded, "I've heard that a lot, especially in the years since the pandemic. It has become a convenient excuse not to attend. But it's a fallacious argument. Certainly the church is the people, but that doesn't mean the people shouldn't gather regularly. And most gatherings will be in a building."

Becky added, "I've had to remind several church members in recent months of Hebrews 10:25: 'And let us not neglect our meeting together, as some people do, but encourage one another, especially now that the day of his return is drawing near.'"

"I don't know why church members are even questioning the importance of worship attendance," Jorge said. "Our community group has been doing a survey of the New Testament. From Acts 2 to Revelation 3, the local church is the focus. And these churches were gathering for worship."

Jorge spoke with such authority that the room was quiet for a few seconds. So he filled the void. "When Paul was fussing at the Corinthian church for their abuse of the Lord's Supper, he started by saying, 'When you meet together . . .' He doesn't say '*if* you meet together,' he says, '*when* you meet together.'"†

---

† 1 Corinthians 11:20.

Oliver was impressed by how conversant both Becky and Jorge were with Scripture. Connection Church might have its challenges with biblical teaching, but it wasn't with the leaders at this meeting.

"Okay," Oliver said, wanting to move the group forward. "I think we're on the same page about the importance of worship attendance. What about community group attendance? Why is that one of the key elements of commitment?"

"I was a member of a church in Charlotte before I moved here," Emma interjected quickly. "They didn't emphasize small groups *or* Sunday school. I never felt connected—kind of like Jill said about *us*. Sure, I got involved in some ministries at the church, but small groups are great if you really want to get to know people."

"My wife and I were already involved in a community group here at Connection before we decided to join the church," Rob said. "Some friends of ours invited us, so we were already connected—and it's made all the difference in the world."

"By the way," Becky added, "none of the inactive or partially active members we interviewed were in a community group. I would say it's not a coincidence that they were inactive or declining in frequency of attendance."

"Wow," Oliver said. "It sounds like small groups are the glue that holds things together by giving people a place to belong within the larger structure of the church."

"And it shows up in the offering plate as well," Becky said with enthusiasm. "I ran some data on giving in the church— which is really easy to do with our church management system. I calculated per-family giving of members who are in community groups versus members *not* in community groups. Get ready for this data point: The community group members' per-family giving was *five times* higher than the others!"

Jorge gave a low whistle. "I had heard there was a statistical difference," he said. "But I had no idea the difference was that significant."

After a brief silence, Oliver asked if anyone had anything to add. When no one spoke up, he said, "Okay, I think we all agree that worship attendance and community group involvement are two very important metrics in our church. Let's look at the next category: involvement in a ministry or program for church members. Becky, can you explain what you mean by this category?"

"Absolutely. We have a lot of ministries and programs here at Connection Church—in fact, probably *too* many. But that's a different conversation. This category refers to those activities that explicitly benefit church members. For example, Jorge is a community group leader and an elder. Those two responsibilities would be in this category since they are largely internal to the church."

"I am very involved in the music ministry of the church," Emma added. "I love our choir, and I love helping to lead music for the children. Those ministries are also largely for the church members."

"Speaking of children," Becky said, "we have more people involved in children's ministry than any other category. From the nursery to fifth grade, there's a lot of activity. We also have decent ministry participation for students sixth grade and up, but it's not as well-staffed as the children's ministry."

"Well," Jorge said, "I can't imagine a church being a church without ministries and programs for its members. Are we ready to move on to the next category?"

There were no objections.

≡

Emma spoke first about the final category Becky had listed. "I was curious about this one," she began. "At one time we had a ministry in Uganda. I went on four different mission trips to Kampala. Would our mission trips be included in ministry beyond the church?"

"Absolutely," Becky responded. "These are the ministries that are largely done to and for those outside of our church. I think Uganda would be considered *outside*."

Everyone laughed.

"It's been a long time since we've had a Uganda mission trip," Jorge commented. "What happened?"

Oliver knew the story well, and it was a sad one.

"Carl and Freida Upshaw started that ministry," he replied. "They had both served as missionaries in East Africa. Then Carl was killed in a tragic auto accident, and Freida moved down to Florida, where her kids are."

"Yeah, I think it was St. Petersburg," Jorge said. "I had forgotten that Carl and Freida were the heart of the Ugandan ministry."

"Sadly, that ministry went away after Carl died," Oliver said.

"What are some other ministries that fit this category?" Emma asked.

"Our food ministry and water bottle ministry to the homeless in downtown Raleigh has six or seven members involved. It would certainly be included," Becky said.

"I have something that *should* be part of this category," Oliver said. "But it's more a matter of *omission* than something we're doing. In fact, I feel it might be the one area in which we're most lacking as a church."

"That sounds serious, Pastor," Jorge said.

"Well, I didn't mean to cast it in such negative terms," Oliver said. "But it *is* important. We're *not* an evangelistic church. We know the Great Commission commands us to go into our community and share the gospel. But we're not doing it. And that's on *me* as your pastor."

"It's something we're all responsible for," Emma said.

"I mean, North Carolina was home to Billy Graham, one of the great evangelists of all time," Oliver continued. "He lived in Montreat, near Asheville. The Cove, the training center he started, is right outside Asheville. The Billy Graham Library is in Charlotte. Billy and Ruth Graham are buried in the prayer garden next to the library."

Oliver hadn't realized how much emotion he felt about the issue. "Maybe one of the key fruits of this task force will be to move our church to reach people in our community with the gospel."

Becky looked at Oliver with surprise. They had worked alongside each other for several years now at the church, and he had never once said anything about evangelism.

Maybe this task force is getting us on the right track after all.

Emma spoke up before Oliver could continue. "This is definitely an issue we need to come back to, Pastor. But I think we should keep moving for now."

Oliver nodded and Emma continued, "Becky, you've done a great job with this analysis. Though I wish we had more than forty-three members who have three or four checkmarks, at least we have those forty-three. Is there anything else we need to know about your data before we begin asking the 'why' questions?"

"I think I have a few more interesting points," Becky responded. "First, almost all of those with only three checks are missing in the "ministry beyond the church" category. There are a few exceptions, of course, but that's a consistent pattern."

"I wish I could say I'm surprised," Oliver said, "but I'm not." He could still feel his heart racing from his earlier comments about Billy Graham.

Becky continued, "A second fascinating discovery is that thirty-six of the forty-three members came to Connection Church from other churches as adults. Only seven of the forty-three have been here all of their adult lives."

"That *is* fascinating," Jorge interjected. "We need to dig down on that point before we leave today, but I want to give you a chance to finish. Do you have any other insights?"

Becky took a deep breath. "This discovery shocked me," she said intensely. "These forty-three people account for 89 percent of our giving."

The room went silent as the group absorbed this new information.

"Wait, will you say that again, Becky?" Jorge wanted to make sure he had heard correctly.

"These forty-three most active members account for 89 percent of our total giving. We have 425 members. We have an average Sunday worship attendance of 206. But 10 percent of our total membership accounts for almost ninety cents of every dollar given."

Emma ran the numbers on her phone's calculator. "So from a pure statistical point of view, we could lose the 382 members not on the list and we would only lose 11 percent of our total giving."

"That is absolutely stunning," Jorge said. He glanced at his phone and said, "I know we agreed to be done no later than 8:00 tonight—and it's 7:53 right now. But if the rest of you are up for it, I'd like to continue for another hour. I feel like we're starting to make some progress."

"But let's take a five-minute break," Oliver added.

All heads nodded affirmatively.

≡

"I have to admit," Oliver said when the meeting reconvened, "I didn't expect the meeting to go this way. I'm not disappointed, just surprised."

He was doing his best to make sense of all this data. He had often said that he wished being a pastor were only about preaching and pastoral care. Most church members had no idea about all the hats a pastor had to wear.

Well, I know where to turn for this one.

"Becky," Oliver continued, "I know you well. You have

obviously thought about these findings beyond the data. Do you have any thoughts or conclusions?"

"Well," Becky said hesitatingly, "I don't want to presume to have the answers. Maybe it's best if we hear from the rest of you first."

Jorge jumped in immediately. "Look," he said with utmost seriousness, "let's not worry about protocol. Becky, if you have some thoughts, let's hear them. We won't hesitate to give our opinions."

"Okay," Becky began. "Our church is neither small nor large. This means we have a lot of variety, but we're not so big that we all can't know almost everyone."

Emma interjected, "That's true, you certainly know the members and the heartbeat of our church."

"Here's what I see," Becky continued. "Most of our committed core of forty-three came from other churches as adults. As I've talked with these people over the years, one thing they seem to have in common is that they came from churches with a high bar."

Jorge interrupted. "Clarify what you mean by 'a high bar,' Becky."

"You can substitute the word *expectations*, or *commitment*, for *bar*," she replied. "So they came from churches that had high expectations of their members."

"This makes so much sense," Oliver said. "Do you all remember 'Great Fight #2'? I think it happened five years ago."

"How could we forget?" Emma responded. "Great Fight #1 was about the name change. Great Fight #2 was about adding a new members class. And, of course, Ken Cassidy was at the forefront of both battles."

"I knew we needed some sort of entry point class where we could provide information and establish expectations for membership," Oliver continued. "I know myself well enough to understand that I can be hesitant to ask or expect people to do things in the church. The class was my attempt to 'raise the bar,' to use Becky's term."

Oliver paused for a few seconds and looked around the room at the other members of the task force. He was blessed to be able to work with such incredible leaders, and he could tell by their faces that they were on board with the direction he was going.

"Here's the bottom line," he said. "I let Ken get his way when he riled up a handful of others to oppose the new members class. I should have stood up to him and accepted the consequences."

Trap #2

Churches have a low bar of expectations for their members, and they have not clearly articulated whatever expectations they have.

"We all could have done better back then," Jorge added. "I knew in my heart that letting Ken get his way was a mistake, and I didn't give you enough support, Oliver."

"Well," Oliver replied, "we are now a low-bar church. That much is clear. If we expect nothing from our people, that's exactly what we'll get."

"And that certainly contributes to a lack of commitment," Emma added. "Pastor, I think it was you who asked the question, 'Where have all the church members gone?' Well, if you don't expect them to show up and be actively involved, they're probably not going to. At least that seems to be the way things are going in today's culture."

Oliver was amazed. He never thought the task force would get this far so soon. He looked over at Becky and could tell what she was thinking by the look on her face. She was concerned that all this information was hurtful to him. He needed to set the record straight.

"Look," Oliver began, "you might be concerned that all of these revelations are hurtful to me. After all, I've been the pastor for the past eight years. But I want all of you to know that what we are discovering is actually *liberating* for me. I knew something was off at our church. I think we all did. Now we are beginning to discover some major traps we've fallen into— traps that could end up killing the church. But that's actually good. It means we can begin praying about them and looking for solutions."

The room was quiet, but not out of awkwardness or pity. In fact, despite the challenges, everyone had more confidence than ever that they could move forward successfully.

But it wouldn't be without some bumps in the road. In fact, unbeknownst to the members of the task force, another meeting was taking place at the same time, where Ken Cassidy was spreading rumors and rallying his troops.

5

THAT MEMBERSHIP THING

OLIVER LEFT THE OFFICE AT 4:00 P.M., which was earlier than usual. He and Melanie had a tradition of celebrating the anniversary of their first date with dinner at their favorite restaurant. Though the celebration didn't come with quite the fanfare of their wedding anniversary, Oliver actually liked it better.

He recalled the first time he ever saw Melanie—the way she walked, the confident tilt to her head, the sparkle of fun in her eye. Though he always encouraged young people to be cautious about "love at first sight," that wasn't advice he could have heeded at seventeen, when he met Melanie. And though few would have guessed that he was an introvert, it had taken a double dose of courage to ask Melanie for that first date.

It's hard to believe I've known her for more than forty years, and that we've been married for thirty-seven, Oliver mused. *And each passing year is a reminder of how much I love her and how great a blessing she is to me.*

There had been some turbulent years, to be sure, about a decade into their marriage; and though for both of them divorce had never been an option, Oliver had to admit there were times when he had wondered whether they might break that commitment.

Though he would never want to face another crisis point in his relationship with Melanie, Oliver believed that their marriage today was stronger because of the difficulties they had navigated when they were younger. He was more deeply committed to her than ever. And he was confident she felt the same way about him.

Their reservation was at Thomas's Steakhouse, which was located in the small downtown area not far from the church. Though they rarely ate steak, it was fun to make an exception every once in a while. Thomas's had quickly become their go-to restaurant for special occasions after it opened five years ago, and Oliver always looked forward to going there.

When he arrived home, Melanie was ready to go, looking especially beautiful in a bright blue dress.

But of course she always looks beautiful to me.

Their reservation was for five o'clock, and Melanie chuckled as she got into the car.

"What's so funny, girl?" Oliver asked with a broad smile.

"We are officially senior citizens," she replied. "We are going out for dinner early with all the old folks."

Oliver wasn't sure why he always looked at the menu after they settled in at the table. He knew exactly what he wanted. Maybe he looked to see if the prices, by some miracle, had gone down. They hadn't.

That's why we only come here two or three times a year.

As usual, they both ordered the small filet mignon. For Melanie, it was always well done, with a butterfly cut. Oliver preferred medium rare, and he had never understood why his wife would choose to ruin such a nice, tender piece of meat.

As they waited for the food to be served, they talked about the kids, the house, and the neighborhood, but then Melanie cut to the chase.

"You seem restless," she said. "It reminds me of the times we've moved. Are you thinking about leaving the church?"

Oliver smiled. It always amazed him how well she could read his moods. She had gotten some of it right this time, but not all of it.

"You are right as always, dear," he said with a grin. "But the restlessness is different this time. I have no desire to leave Connection. I think God is doing something about my leadership here. It may seem weird, but I think my calling is to make Connection Church a new church, rather than us leaving to go somewhere else."

"Is this restlessness the result of the Vision Task Force?" Melanie asked.

"Yes and no. I think I was feeling unsettled already, and my restlessness led me to start the group. But then some of the things we've uncovered have also been unsettling. So the task force didn't *cause* my restlessness, but it hasn't exactly relieved it either."

They paused as the server brought the food. Oliver was hungry, and the steak looked delicious. At the server's request, they both cut into their steaks. And in unison, they both said, "Perfect!"

Oliver thoroughly enjoyed the first bite of his filet mignon, but then he wanted to finish his thoughts about the task force.

"I would say the task force has exacerbated my restlessness. But I'm gaining greater clarity about my leadership and the future of the church."

Melanie smiled as Oliver concluded, "But enough about work. Let's enjoy these fine filets while they're still perfect."

≡

Becky had scheduled an appointment to meet with Oliver at eight o'clock the next morning. She typically would put something on his calendar whenever she felt she needed thirty minutes or longer. By mutual agreement they always met in the small conference room with glass on three sides whenever their meeting was closed-door.

Even first thing in the morning, Oliver was confident that Becky would come to the meeting with her usual trifecta of optimism, enthusiasm, and determination. And she typically began these meetings with the same three words.

"I've been thinking," Becky said as Oliver tried to subdue his smile. "The other night, we talked a lot about commitment or lack of commitment, and we looked at the forty-three most committed members in our church. Of those forty-three, thirty-six came from other churches."

Oliver simply nodded. He didn't want to interrupt her train of thought.

"I haven't gotten to all thirty-six yet, but I've heard from most of them. I ask them a simple question, 'Did you go through a required membership class before joining your former church?'"

Becky paused for effect.

"Okay," Oliver pressed her. "What did you find?"

She smiled as if she had discovered a treasure trove. "Every person thus far has said *yes*."

"Everyone?"

"One hundred percent," she said with satisfaction.

"Wow," Oliver responded. "I know that researchers say correlation does not prove causation, but this is incredibly valuable information."

"Now think about the second biggest fight our church has had since you arrived."

"Oh my goodness, you're right," Oliver said softly. "Ken led a faction of the church to oppose the idea of starting a new members class. He yelled at me about legalism and control, and I caved. I was weak."

Becky smiled. "Don't be so hard on yourself. Anyway, as the Vision Task Force continues to do its work, I can see this step becoming a major part of our future. We really need to have an entry point where the church supplies information and sets forth expectations."

"Wait a second, Becky. Repeat that last sentence."

Becky thought for a moment and repeated it almost verbatim. "We need to have an entry point where the church provides information and sets forth expectations."

"Wow!" Oliver said. "I think you're on to something. Last time we proposed a membership class to the church, we never talked about *expectations*, only about giving information."

"Well," Becky replied, "we never talked about expectations with the congregation, but we did talk about it as leaders. You may remember that we talked about using a pledge we got from a book on church membership."

"A pledge?" Oliver was having trouble recalling.

"Yes," Becky said. "Here it is."

She handed Oliver a sheet of paper. He read the words slowly:

I am a believer and a church member.

Being a Christian means believing in a set of biblical truths. I cannot consider myself a follower of Christ unless I embrace the truths he gave us.

I am a disciple and a church member.

Being a Christian and a church member also means following Christ in our actions. It's asking the question "What would Jesus do?" and acting accordingly. I cannot consider myself a follower of Christ unless I have a faith that works.

I am a serving church member.

Being a Christian means desiring to emulate the servanthood of Jesus, particularly through my church. After all, he said that he came to serve and not to be served (Mark 10:45). I cannot consider myself a follower of Christ unless I am willing to serve others in my church and beyond.

I am a witnessing church member.

Being a Christian means obeying Jesus' commandment, uttered as he prepared to leave the earth, to make disciples of all nations. I cannot consider myself a follower of Christ unless I am witnessing to what I have seen and sharing the gospel with others.

I am a praying church member.

We remember, too, how Jesus prayed, how he agonized in prayer, and how he pleaded with his disciples to pray. He even taught them how to pray in the verses we now call the Lord's Prayer (Matthew 6:9-13). I cannot consider myself a follower of Christ and a functioning church member unless I am one who prays.

I am a committed church member.

Our belief in Christ and our obedience to Christ are meant to be lived out in the community of the local church. We cannot miss that biblical truth. Church membership, faithful attendance, and local church ministry are neither optional nor legalistic. While belonging to a church does not save me, I am reminded throughout the New Testament, from Acts 2 to Revelation 3, that this large portion of Scripture is written to and about local churches.

Being a Christian and serving in a local church is how we live out and express our joy in being forgiven and saved by grace.

I am a Christian, and I am a church member.

And I thank God that I am.[†]

"That's awesome," Oliver said. "I really like that. We need to establish that church membership *means* something, so that people will understand clearly what we expect of everyone who joins with us."

≡

Jorge stopped by the church the next day to see Oliver. He ran into Becky in the hallway. She was also on her way to see the pastor.

When Becky poked her head into Oliver's office and asked whether he had time to meet with her and Jorge, he welcomed them in.

"I hate to drop in unexpected," Jorge said, "but this will take

---

† Adapted from Thom S. Rainer, *I Am a Christian* (Carol Stream, IL: Tyndale Momentum, 2022), 109–111.

only a minute. I want to share some details of the membership class fiasco with you."

"This sounds interesting," Oliver replied. "What do you have?"

"When Ken led the revolt a few years ago," Jorge began, "he used two very specific arguments to claim you were overstepping your authority."

"I don't remember them, Jorge," Becky interjected. "I guess I was more focused on the emotions and relationships at the time."

"Neither do I," Oliver added. "Please, enlighten us both."

"First of all, Ken claimed we were 'changing the rules in the middle of the game' by adding a new members class," Jorge said. "We were asking all existing members to accept a new standard that was different from what was in place when they joined. Ken even used the phrase 'bait and switch.'"

"Yeah, I remember now," Oliver responded. "We wanted to make sure all the members were together, that we were all on the same page. We didn't want two different classes of church members."

"Well," Jorge said frankly, "I think that was a mistake."

Oliver raised his eyebrows, but said nothing. He waited for Jorge to explain.

"I came across these statistics only recently," Jorge continued. "Without any additions to the congregation, attendance will drop by almost one-third every year in a typical American church."

Oliver and Becky looked at the data on a sheet of paper Jorge had handed them.

"These numbers are amazing! Challenging, but amazing," Becky said with excitement.

Oliver laughed. There was no question that Becky loved data.

"A typical church loses one person per year to death for every one hundred in average attendance," she read from the print-out. "They lose nine per hundred from people moving out of the community, and another seven per hundred from members leaving to go to another church in the community. And from some members attending less often, the average church loses fifteen per one hundred in attendance."

Becky perused the numbers again. "The data is stunning," she reiterated. "A church has to replace thirty-two church members for every one hundred in attendance—*every year*—just to stay even with where they were! Since our church has an average attendance of *two* hundred, we have to replace sixty-four people each year. Where have all the *church members* gone? This data alone explains most of it."

"I understand the numbers, Jorge," Oliver said slowly, "but I'm not sure what this has to do with a new members class."

"Look at it this way: In any church, you are regularly adding members and losing members. Over time, the newer members become the majority."

"I get it!" Becky exclaimed. "We don't have to require existing members to go through the new members class. We simply have to establish higher expectations with our new members, and over time they will naturally replace the longer-term members and we'll end up with a higher-expectation church."

"Exactly," Jorge said. "The process is called *grandfathering*. Longer-term members always have the option to attend the new members class, but they don't have to. But since all new members *will* be required to attend the class, over time the church will become more like the newer members. They will begin to set a higher standard for membership."

"So if we had compromised on this point, Ken would have lost one of his major arguments," Oliver replied, shaking his head. "I mean, it's not ideal, but it's better than dividing the church."

"I promised I would only take a few minutes," Jorge said, "so let me briefly address the second issue that divided the church."

"Go ahead."

"Ken showed them all the material they would have to learn," Jorge continued. "And he discouraged them by emphasizing the amount of time the new members class would take. If you recall, we were talking about six hours split over three nights."

Oliver thought he knew where Jorge was headed with this, but he waited for him to continue.

"The breadth of material we were proposing for the new members class was just too much for a starting point," Jorge said. "And asking people to give up three evenings is a non-starter for many people. We really need to consolidate and simplify the material, focus on the most important points, and offer it in a single session—maybe a two-hour block."

"That makes complete sense," Becky said.

Oliver was excited to feel some momentum beginning to build.

"So if we consistently teach the basic truths of Scripture, establish clear expectations for our members, and communicate those expectations to all new, incoming members, it won't be long before this church is thriving again. I can *feel* it."

Trap #3

Church members (and nonmembers) do not understand or embrace the biblical meaning of church membership.

≡

After Jorge and Becky left his office, Oliver marveled at the timing of their visit. That very morning, he had been preparing a new sermon series from 1 Corinthians 12–14, titled "What Does It Mean to Be a Member of a Church?" Their interruption gave him a clearer sense of direction and a greater enthusiasm to dig deeper.

He read through 1 Corinthians 12 again, though he knew the background of the chapter well. The people in the church at Corinth were divided over many issues. The apostle Paul, in his letter, is specifically dealing with the abuse and misunderstanding of spiritual gifts in the church. He addresses the problem by reminding the church members that all spiritual gifts come from the Holy Spirit, and that no gift is superior to any other.

Paul uses the metaphor of the human body to describe the church. He emphasizes how the parts of the body—including the hands, ears, eyes, nose, head, and feet—must work together in order for the body to function properly. The whole body suffers if one member is not functioning well, or at all.

Oliver had six Bible translations open before him. Some used the word *member* to describe the parts of the body; two used the synonym *part*. Oliver preferred *member* because of its direct application to church membership.

He knew that many church members—and maybe *most* of the members at Connection Church—viewed church membership as similar to other types of membership, such as membership in a country club or civic organization.

"But church membership is different," Oliver said aloud. "It's all about what each person can do for the greater body. It's about serving before being served."

He reread the pledge that Becky had copied for him. He particularly like this part of the pledge:

I am a serving church member.
   Being a Christian means desiring to emulate the
   servanthood of Jesus, particularly through my church.
   After all, he said that he came to serve and not to be
   served. I cannot consider myself a follower of Christ
   unless I am willing to serve others in my church and
   beyond.

He knew that a single sermon series would not reverse years of self-serving church membership, but it was a start, one of many strategies to address the issue of members' not grasping the biblical meaning of church membership.

Oliver knew that this sermon series was also a step toward

solving the problem of failing to train people in the essential truths of Scripture. He would make certain to dig deeply into the text, and he knew it would point to such foundational truths as salvation through Christ alone, the Atonement, and others.

Despite the roller coaster of events and emotions over the past several years, which had come to a head in the unsettled feelings he had experienced recently, he could sense that the overall trajectory was now healthy. It was a new beginning and a fresh start.

Oliver had set his phone aside to focus on his study of 1 Corinthians 12. When he decided to take a break, he saw two missed phone calls from Emma and a voicemail she had left.

He had been planning to call her anyway, to bring her up to speed on the conversation he'd had with Jorge and Becky that morning; so he decided to call her back now.

First he listened to Emma's voicemail: "Oliver, this issue is not really urgent, but it is important. Please call me back as soon as you can."

Oliver wasn't comfortable with the tone of Emma's voice. Something was wrong. He returned call her immediately, and she answered on the first ring.

"Hey, Emma," he said, "I got your voicemail. What's up?"

"Hey, Oliver," she responded somberly. "We have a problem."

Oliver waited for her to explain.

"It's Ken," she said bluntly. "He's causing more trouble than ever."

6

THE UPRISING

OLIVER WAS SHAKEN BY EMMA'S CALL. He hated it that Ken always affected him that way. He knew that he spent too much emotional energy on him. Just seeing Ken or hearing his name evoked a visceral response.

Instead of coming to the church, Emma suggested they meet at Pirkle's, a small coffee shop just outside the downtown area. Emma told Oliver that she didn't want Becky to be a part of this initial conversation. She knew that Becky wasn't likely to happen into Pirkle's.

When Oliver arrived, Emma was at a table, waiting. He ordered a vanilla cappuccino and sat down. There were only a few other people in the shop, since it was the middle of the afternoon, so Emma and Oliver could have a conversation without being overheard.

"I have to admit that my gut is churning," he began. "You said two things that hit me hard. One, that Ken is on a rampage for some reason. And two, that you didn't think Becky should be here. That seemed like an odd stipulation."

Oliver knew Emma well. She would get right to the point.

"Oliver," Emma replied, "have you met the CEO of my company? Her name is Lisa Clowder."

Oliver had to think. "Only once, if I recall correctly," he replied. "You asked me to give a dedicatory blessing for your new facility. I spoke with Lisa briefly. Seemed like a nice lady." Oliver wasn't sure where Emma was going with this conversation.

"In my role as chief operating officer," Emma continued, "I have responsibility for the day-to-day operations of the company. But part of my job is also deciding what information Lisa needs to know. I want her fully informed, but she doesn't need to worry about every little thing. We have a big company, and I must serve as her filter."

Emma took a sip of her drink.

"Though I am not on staff at the church," she said, "I try to show respect for your leadership in the same way I would otherwise. And I would only come to you if I thought the issue was important."

"And the issue is Ken, right?" Oliver asked.

"Yes, it's Ken—but it's not *just* Ken."

Emma took another sip before continuing the conversation.

"Every organization has some negative people, and churches are no exception. On the other hand, I have heard more concerns from people in the church lately, and I've gotten more calls about various issues than at any other point I can remember. The common denominator seems to be Ken, at the forefront of this negativity, but he seems to have some traction this time."

"Can you give me an example of what you're talking about?" Oliver asked.

"Sure," Emma said quickly. "He has resurrected the church-membership-class issue. He has some people worried that you're about to impose strict standards and expectations on the members in a legalistic way. It's basically his argument from a few years ago. But he's leveraging his attendance at our first task force meeting to bolster his credibility."

Oliver shook his head, and Emma paused to take a breath. She knew he would be upset by what she said next.

"The new issue," she said much more slowly, "is his claim that Becky is not working. She is, for lack of a better word, *goofing off.*"

"Oh, for Pete's sake!" Oliver exclaimed. "Where in the world is *that* coming from? You know that Becky is an incredibly hard worker."

"I really don't know the basis of the rumor, Oliver," Emma responded. "But the rumor is making the rounds. Though I know you're loath to meet with him, I really think you should. The gossip and negativity have to stop."

Oliver took a deep breath and saw that his phone was ringing. He was getting ready to ignore it when he saw that Ken was the caller.

"Speaking of the—"

Oliver was glad he had caught himself in time. Ken didn't deserve to be called the devil. Emma smiled and gave him a knowing look.

Oliver took the call. The conversation was very brief.

"He wants to meet with me," Oliver said. "And he's bringing along Ted Brimley—remember him? I'm sure he wants a witness."

"Ah, yes, I remember Ted," Emma said ruefully. "We were in the same community group. He wasn't that active, but he caused his share of trouble. I thought he left the church."

Emma took another sip of her coffee, though Oliver was thinking it couldn't possibly still be hot.

"Look, Oliver," Emma said emphatically. "You should probably have a witness there too."

"Would you be willing to come?" Oliver asked. "We're meeting in my office at 7:00 tonight."

"That's not a good idea," Emma responded, catching Oliver off guard. "I don't want to make an issue out of this, but there's no doubt that Ken is uncomfortable with women leaders. I think my presence would be a hindrance. You need Jorge there."

Oliver sighed and sent a quick text to Jorge. "I think he said he was in meetings this afternoon. But I'm sure he'll get back to me."

≡

Oliver got to the church at 6:15. He hoped Jorge would also arrive early to discuss the situation, and he was not disappointed. Within ten minutes, the two men were speculating about Ken's agenda.

At ten to seven, they heard footsteps in the hallway. Oliver and Jorge stood to greet Ken and Ted with a handshake, but neither man offered his hand. Instead, Ken pointed at Jorge and snapped, "What's *he* doing here?"

"I invited him," Oliver responded calmly.

"Well, you didn't ask me!" Ken was almost yelling.

"Ken, you didn't ask me about Ted, either," Oliver responded with a confident voice. "We are here to hear from you. Can we get started?"

Ken pulled out a sheet of paper.

Good grief, Oliver thought. *He has a list.*

"The first issue," he began caustically, "is an old problem popping up again. Word has it that you are planning to commandeer the church again through a new members class. You tried this once before, and it failed."

There was so much wrong with Ken's opening statement, but Oliver and Jorge knew this wasn't the time to refute his claims. Ken was clearly looking for an argument, but Oliver and Jorge had agreed to listen only.

Ken seemed taken aback by their silence, but he pressed on to point number two.

"Second," he said, his voice still sharp with indignation, "our pastor is not taking care of the members. In fact, he is being rude to them."

Though Jorge wasn't planning to speak, he chose to interject at this point.

"Ken," he said evenly, "can you give me a specific example?"

"I sure can," Ken replied. "Susan Brohm said that she asked you for some help, Pastor, and you told her you didn't have time for her."

Oliver suppressed a smile. He was surprised that he found the accusation humorous.

Who in the world is Susan Brohm? He had never heard that name before.

What Oliver most wanted to hear were the charges against Becky. It didn't take long for Ken to comply.

"Third," he said, continuing down his checklist, "we are paying Becky Garner a good salary, but she hardly ever works. People are saying that when they come by to see her in the office, she is never around. To my way of thinking, that makes her not a good worker, and she's cheating the church."

Oliver could feel his face flush. He looked over at Jorge, who shook his head ever so slightly to keep the pastor from responding.

"Who are these 'people who are saying'?" Jorge asked bluntly, putting extra emphasis on the last four words.

Ken was a bully, but he knew he couldn't bully Jorge. Instead, he went on to his other complaints. But it was obvious that the first three issues were his main focus.

Ken concluded his recitation with an announcement that took both Jorge and Oliver by surprise.

"Our annual congregational meeting is in two weeks. Just giving you fair warning: I plan on moving for the dismissal of both Pastor Wagner and Becky Garner. I have the right to make this motion."

After that mic-drop moment, Ken strode out of the office, followed by Ted Brimley, who hadn't said a word the entire meeting.

"Well, that was enlightening," Oliver concluded after the two men had gone.

≡

The next morning, Oliver met with Becky to let her know what Ken had said. She wasn't bothered by it.

"To be honest, I'm not that worried about my position at Connection Church. I've learned to hold all things loosely and just trust God for the outcome. And while I don't expect Ken to be able to force me out, I have total peace regardless of what happens."

When Oliver told her about the accusation that he had been rude to Susan Brohm, she laughed.

"I'm not surprised you don't remember her, Oliver. She only came for three or four weeks right after the lockdown ended. But she never joined. It almost seemed as if she had a mission to criticize the church. But I think she saw that she wouldn't get anywhere with that approach here. I know it sounds bad, but I was actually relieved when she stopped coming."

That evening, at home, when Oliver shared the news about Ken with Melanie, she remarked on his emotions.

"I have to say I'm surprised—and pleased—by how calm you are, honey. Usually, you would be quite upset about this level of negativity in the church."

"I'm surprising myself," Oliver responded. "Maybe I'm finally growing up after all these years. When I told you I thought my calling was to make Connection Church a new church, rather than us leaving to go somewhere else, I was serious. God is doing a work in this congregation, and I have to expect that the process will include some conflict and spiritual warfare."

Over the next two weeks, there was a flurry of activity leading up to the annual meeting. Jorge called an elders' meeting to let them know what to expect from Ken. The elders were good and godly men. They knew Ken, and they knew their pastor, and they assured Oliver they would have his back at the meeting.

One morning, when Oliver arrived at the church, there was

a note taped to his office chair. It simply read, "You know we're praying. —Frances. Ephesians 6:12."

Oliver smiled as he carefully removed the tape and put the note inside the front cover of his Bible. Then he looked up the Scripture passage—even though he had long since committed it to memory.

We are not fighting against flesh-and-blood enemies, but against evil rulers and authorities of the unseen world, against mighty powers in this dark world, and against evil spirits in the heavenly places.

Oliver felt a surge of confidence knowing that Frances and the other members of the intercessory prayer team were "on the job," as they liked to say. This tight-knit group of eight to ten people had been praying for the church every day for years—maybe even decades by now.

I know they were praying long before I got here, Oliver said to himself.

Though mostly they prayed over the phone with each other, or by text, they met together in person three times in the days leading up to the annual meeting. And they were doing more than just meeting. They were in a battle of spiritual warfare, tearing down the strongholds of the enemy through prayer. Although Ken Cassidy and the other members he had rallied were the faces of the troublemakers, the intercessors were not confused about who the *true* enemy was.

≡

Janet Dickinson was the elected moderator, serving the second year of a three-year term. Oliver thought she had been an excellent choice. She had a great temperament, she was always fair, and she truly liked people. Her smile was genuine, and it could be disarming in tense situations.

If ever there was a tense situation, Oliver thought as he left his office to head to the meeting, *it is this meeting tonight.*

Though he should not have been surprised, Oliver wasn't prepared for how full the worship center was. He estimated at least 250 people had shown up for the meeting—well above the average Sunday morning attendance.

Jorge greeted Oliver with a slap on the back. "You're probably thinking the same thing I am, Oliver: *Who are all these people?*"

Becky joined them at the front of the room. "It looks like we have about 275 people in the room," she said confidently. "As far as I can tell, they're all members of the church. Some have not attended in months, maybe years, but I don't think any nonmembers are here."

"So are you recommending that we forgo any steps to confirm membership?" Jorge asked.

"Correct," Becky responded. "I think we should move forward with an affirmed quorum of members. No need to stir up anything else. I already told Janet to proceed when she's ready."

Just as Becky mentioned Janet's name, the moderator called the meeting to order.

"I have been informed that we have a quorum of our members," Janet said. "We will proceed with our agenda."

Though the atmosphere was noticeably tense, most of the meeting was routine—minutes, finances, membership, facilities. Everyone was waiting for the third-to-last item: new business.

When the time came, Janet's voice maintained the same calm and even tone she had employed throughout the meeting, "We are now ready for new business. Beyond approval of the budget, the leadership of the church has no new business. Is there any new business from the floor?"

The air felt thick. The next few seconds were like an eternity as no one said a word. Then Ken spoke up in an overly loud voice from the back of the room.

"Yes, I have a motion for new business."

"Very well," responded Janet. "The chair recognizes Ken Cassidy. Please come to the front and state your motion at the microphone, Ken."

The room was eerily quiet as Ken walked forward.

"My motion is simple," Ken said. "I move that the church dismiss Pastor Oliver Wagner and our administrative director, Becky Garner. I am presenting this motion as one and I do not wish to divide it."

"I second," Ted Brimley shouted from the back of the room. Many of the members seated near the front looked with confusion toward the back. It was obvious they didn't know who Ted was.

Becky looked at Oliver, and Emma looked at Jorge. They knew exactly what Ken was doing. Any negative votes against either Oliver or Becky would be added together in a single motion. In other words, even if someone were only against one of them, he or she would be voting against both.

Janet was unfazed. She calmly continued, "Very well, we have a motion for the dismissal of our pastor and our administrative director. According to the bylaws, the dismissal motion is in order, but if the motion passes, it requires a second vote within two weeks. The motion will carry only with a super-majority of two-thirds of those present."

She paused for a moment. "I am, however, concerned that a single motion for two dismissals is not in order."

Ken looked ready to pounce, but Janet continued before he could say a word.

"I will ask the two parties who are addressed by the motion to state whether they will agree to combine the two questions into a single motion."

Becky looked at Oliver and he nodded affirmatively. She nodded in reply.

Oliver said, "Ms. Moderator, Becky and I are both okay with a single motion."

"Okay," Janet said. She looked as if she might lose her composure for once, but she quickly regained her poise and continued the proceedings.

"Ken," she said, perhaps a bit tersely, "would you like to speak to the motion?"

"Yes, of course I would." Ken pulled out four typewritten pages. He was ready.

For the next several minutes, it was the same narrative Ken had been presenting for years. Oliver was trying to control the church by adding a new members class. And he was not being pastoral, or kind, to church members—though Ken gave no specifics. And Becky was not doing her job. Ken's demeanor suggested he was certain he had wowed the room.

Janet asked, "Is there anyone else who would like to speak to the motion?"

Silence. No one. Not even Ted Brimley.

At this point, Janet breathed an audible sigh of relief. Apparently, nobody—not a single person—wanted to speak against Oliver or Becky. And no one could have been prepared for what happened next.

"Would anyone like to speak against the motion?" she asked.

It was if she had opened the floodgates after a hard rain. Almost simultaneously, more than one hundred people were on their feet, pressing forward toward the microphone and quickly forming a line that snaked around the perimeter of the room. An additional hundred were on their feet in their pews, standing up for their pastor, standing up for Becky, standing up for their church.

"If we give everyone a turn at the mic," Janet said, "we will need to bring in some sleeping bags."

The crowd roared with laughter.

Janet looked over at Jorge, who was standing on the front row.

"As a respected elder and longtime member of our church, would you like to speak first?"

Jorge nodded and stepped over to the microphone.

"Folks," he said with quiet authority, "I could present an impassioned defense of Oliver and Becky. But you already know these charges against them are false, because you know their hearts, their work ethic, their love of this church, and their love of Christ. We need to let them know we support them, we love them, and we are honored to have these two servants in our church."

Jorge paused to regain his composure.

"I don't want to presume upon each one of you who desires to speak against the motion, but if you will allow me, I'm going to call for the question so we can get to the business of voting our support for these two fine leaders."

Janet did not miss a beat. "We have a motion to call the question, which would end all discussion and move us to a vote." The motion passed unanimously by vocal assent. Even Ken did not voice opposition.

"Now," Janet said, "if everyone will return to their seats, it's time for us to vote on the motion of dismissal against Pastor Wagner and Becky Garner. Because this vote is of serious import, I will ask for a formal tally. If you are on the end of a row, the ushers will give you a piece of paper to count those who are standing on your row."

Once the papers had been distributed, Janet continued, "All in favor of the motion—which means you are in favor of dismissing our pastor and Becky—please stand."

A formal tally was hardly necessary, as only seven people stood in support of the motion: Ken and Marilyn Cassidy, Ted Brimley, and four others at the back of the room. Notably, Ted's wife, Katherine, did not stand with him.

Janet smiled. "Okay, you may be seated. Now all those voting against the motion, please stand."

Once again, the assembled members rose to their feet almost as one. The tallies were taken and the sheets passed to the front. Emma helped Janet with the final computations.

"On the question of whether to dismiss Pastor Oliver Wagner and Becky Garner, the motion fails by a vote of 262 to 7."

The applause was immediate and thunderous. Oliver hugged Melanie. Becky hugged her husband, Tim. There were hugs and high fives throughout the room.

Unable to restore order, Janet asked for a motion to end the meeting. Jorge heard her request and made the motion. Another elder seconded. Janet declared the meeting adjourned.

It may have been one of the happiest days in the history of Connection Church.

≡

Oliver and Melanie stayed at the church for almost two hours after the meeting ended. They were understandably exhausted, but they wanted to celebrate a major moment in the history of the church with the people they loved. If Oliver had ever had any doubts about whether the church was behind him, they were put to rest tonight. It had taken several years to build that level of trust, but the time and effort were all worth it for the fruits of his labor that he was now enjoying.

As the last people left the building, Oliver and Melanie walked out hand in hand, feeling so much gratitude—for each other and for the church.

Oliver knew that tonight's victory was more of a beginning than an end. But having seen the level of support he had within the congregation, he was optimistic that his vision of a new church—with the same name, in the same location, with (mostly) the same members—was a possibility.

But there was much work yet to be done.

7

THE NO-GO CHURCH

OLIVER DIDN'T USUALLY SLEEP past six thirty, but at seven o'clock on the morning after the big meeting, he was still in bed. He was exhausted. His body was sore. Until today, he hadn't realized how tense he had been.

Melanie greeted him with the same smile that had captivated him for four decades.

"I tried to be quiet so you could get some rest," she said. "But what are your plans for today? Are you going to the church?"

"No," Oliver replied. "Last night, I rescheduled the only appointment on my calendar for today, and instead I'm taking the day to pray, read my Bible, and ask God where he wants Connection Church to go. Since it's such a pretty day outside,

I think I'll hike part of the Neuse River Trail and look for a place where I can sit for a while."

"That's a great idea," Melanie said. "Is this because of the business meeting last night?"

"Yes and no," Oliver responded thoughtfully. "As I've shared with you before, I sense God is leading us to transform Connection Church into a *new* church. That's been on my mind for a while. But the meeting last night was decisive. Our Vision Task Force has already discovered three traps we've fallen into as a church—not teaching the truths of Scripture clearly enough; not expecting enough of our members; and not clearly establishing the importance of church membership. I feel certain there's another issue, but I need time to gain some clarity on it. A day on the trail will be good for me."

Melanie didn't hesitate. "Let me pack you a lunch and some extra water."

≡

Oliver drove to an access point near the trail. He had a backpack with the food and water Melanie had packed, along with his Bible and the journal in which he had been jotting notes during his morning times of reading and prayer. His goal was to hike for a while to clear his mind, and then find a comfortable place to sit where he could write out his thoughts for further reflection.

For almost an hour, he walked and prayed. Beneath the canopy of trees shading the riverbank, he sensed God's nearness.

Along the way, he came across a group of picnic tables, and he was happy to see they were all vacant. Though he didn't mind being around people, he really needed this time to focus on God and the future of Connection Church.

As he settled in at one of the tables, the first thing he wanted to do was review the hidden traps that he and the task force had identified that were undermining Connection Church. Because so much had transpired in such a short time, he had not taken the time to reflect on them. He pulled out his phone to review the notes he had taken.

> Too many people at Connection either do not believe the Bible or do not understand the basic truths of the Bible, because we have failed to teach the foundational truths of Scripture.

He remembered his initial shock when this trap was revealed. He had always thought that Connection Church was a church that loved the Bible, and that he had been faithfully teaching the Bible there for the past eight years. He wasn't sure how much of the disconnect was due to lack of information or just plain disbelief. Regardless, he knew the issue had to be addressed clearly and without equivocation—and it was his responsibility to lead the way.

He had already begun changing his preaching approach. It was subtle, and not many church members seemed to notice at first. He made a point of explaining the biblical texts and contexts more clearly and more often. He made sure that his preaching had a strong teaching element every week. He focused not only on application of the truth, but also more intentionally on teaching the basic truths of the faith that undergirded everything.

After the third Sunday preaching with this slightly different approach, he began to hear some comments about his sermons. Some said they were learning a lot. Some said his preaching seemed more powerful. They couldn't explain it as much as they could sense it.

Oliver knew it would take longer than three weeks for him to become a more effective preacher, but he was determined in God's power to continue down this path. He also knew the church could make other changes to address this issue, but he would wait until the next task force meeting to get other input.

He turned his attention to the second item in his notes.

Our church has a low bar of expectations for our members, and we have not clearly articulated the expectations we have.

Becky's input about the most committed members of Connection Church had really stunned Oliver when he first heard it. One hundred percent of the most-committed members of the church had gone through a new members class at another church before they came to Connection Church.

Oliver reflected upon those thoughts. *Our most committed*

members learned about commitment somewhere else. That speaks volumes about us!

Oliver had already decided to introduce a new members class to the church. If he hadn't let Ken Cassidy intimidate him a few years ago, the class would be running well by now, and the church would likely have more committed members—and members who were more committed. But he could not dwell on the past. It was time to lead a new church.

> Our members (and nonmembers) do not understand or embrace the biblical meaning of church membership.

As Oliver looked at his note about the third trap, he began to see how much it overlapped with the other two. He knew that a new members class would be the starting point to communicate the vital truths about church membership. It made perfect sense.

"People will learn the essence of biblical church membership as they commit to the church through this foundational class," he said aloud with conviction.

He remembered the conviction he himself had felt while reading the pledge that Becky had brought in. It was essentially a covenant of membership. It was biblical. And it stirred him greatly. Perhaps it would stir others as well.

Though he knew all these ideas would take time to develop, he was ready to move forward. He had been a pastor and a leader long enough to know that there would highs and lows, wins and losses, and undoubtedly some resistance as he led Connection toward becoming a new church in the same location.

≡

Oliver realized he was getting hungry, and he unwrapped the sandwich Melanie had packed for him. As he began to eat, he opened his journal to review the notes he had taken over the past several weeks. He had set himself an ambitious goal of reading through the entire New Testament with an eye for discerning lessons to be learned for the local church. He saw it as a way to keep the big picture in view, even as he was drilling down on specifics during his weekly sermon preparation.

His eye fell on the ideas he had jotted while reading Matthew 9:36-38, and he opened his Bible to read the passage again.

When he saw the crowds, he had compassion on them because they were confused and helpless, like sheep without a shepherd. He said to his disciples, "The harvest is great, but the workers are few. So pray to the Lord who is in charge of the harvest; ask him to send more workers into his fields."

Three things in particular stood out to him as he read. First, his "field" was not some far-flung place. It was simply the streets and neighborhoods surrounding the Connection Church campus—and beyond that, the rest of Rolesville.

Next, it was a reminder that the problem was not a lack of people to reach. Not only were there many people to reach, but they were ready to hear the gospel. The harvest could indeed be great.

There are literally thousands of people in our community, most within a few miles of our campus, who are sheep without a shepherd. Some may be Christians, but most probably are not.

Third, the role of believers was to get out into the harvest field and reach the unreached. Jesus said it powerfully and clearly: The greatest need was for more workers in the harvest field.

Oliver's emotions caught him by surprise. He felt tears run down his cheeks.

My role is to get Connection Church into the harvest field to share the gospel of Christ. If we're obedient, God will take care of the harvest.

Oliver knew that some of his tears were tears of sorrow. He had not led his church to reach people for the gospel. Indeed, he had not done much himself. Simply stated, Connection Church was not evangelistic. He himself had not been evangelistic. They were supposed to go, but they were a no-go church. That would have to change.

I've probably read these verses a hundred times, but now it seems as if the Holy Spirit is saying it's high time we apply them at Connection Church.

Oliver also knew that some of the tears were tears of joy. The opportunity was there in the harvest fields. The future of Connection Church would be great because it was God's future.

Next, Oliver looked at his notes for Mark 1:17-18, where Jesus calls his first disciples. He flipped the pages of his Bible over to Mark.

> Jesus called out to them, "Come and follow me, and
> I will show you how to fish for people!" And they left
> their nets at once and followed him.

Again the passage was very familiar. Again he was seeing it in a new light.

"This is amazing," Oliver said aloud. "When Jesus calls Simon and Andrew, the very first disciples, he not only calls them to *follow* him, but he also calls them to be *evangelistic*. How have I missed that? The call to follow Jesus is one and the same with the call to evangelize."

Oliver marveled at Simon and Andrew's obedience. Not only had they followed Jesus, but they had followed him *immediately*. "They not only gave up their homes, their jobs, and their earthly security to follow him, but they did it without looking back. How can we even hope to come close to that level of commitment?"

Oliver had placed many sticky notes in his Bible. The last one was affixed near the very familiar passage of Acts 1:8. It was as far as he'd gotten in his New Testament study. He decided to add the verse to his journal, directly below Mark 1:17-18.

You will receive power when the Holy Spirit comes upon you. And you will be my witnesses, telling people about me everywhere—in Jerusalem, throughout Judea, in Samaria, and to the ends of the earth.

What fascinated him about Mark 1:17-18 and Acts 1:8 was the promise that God would be with the followers of Jesus as they became fishers of people. In Mark, it was Jesus himself, God in the flesh, who was with them. In Acts, it was the Holy Spirit who would continue to empower them and be present for them.

Oliver's eyes shifted between the two passages. His mind was racing.

"These verses together are amazing. Jesus called his very first disciples to the ministry of evangelism. Then his last words on earth before he ascended were calling his followers to be *witnesses*. I never realized the priority our Savior set on evangelism. It was on his lips from beginning to end in his earthly ministry."

For a brief moment, Oliver felt a cloud of discouragement settle over his mind. He had been in ministry for *decades* without ever focusing on evangelism. In his eight years at Connection Church, he hadn't led the people in any meaningful way to share their faith. He had been so busy doing *good* things that he had neglected the *greatest* thing.

As if sent from heaven, the words of Romans 8:1-2 came to mind, chasing away the doldrums.

So now there is no condemnation for those who belong to Christ Jesus. And because you belong to him, the power of the life-giving Spirit has freed you from the power of sin that leads to death.

Trap #4

Churches fail to obey Christ's command to reach non-Christians with the gospel.

Oliver shook his head in amazement as the phrase "the life-giving Spirit has freed you" jumped out at him. He knew he could not change the past, but he was *free* and *empowered* to lead the church forward from this point on.

Oliver paused to pray. He thanked God for the new clarity surrounding his Word. He thanked God for the opportunity to repent of past shortcomings and move forward into a new day. And he asked God for wisdom and strength for the journey.

≡

Before packing up and heading for home, Oliver wanted to encapsulate how Connection Church might move forward with this new God-given vision. For now, he wanted to keep it simple. Looking back at the three verses he had written in his notebook, he jotted down three words that came to mind: *pray*, *know*, and *go*. Little did he know that those three words would become powerful beacons of light for the members of Connection Church in the days ahead.

Connection Church had had a prayer ministry for years, and it included some of the most devoted members of the church. They prayed for Oliver and the Sunday service every week. They prayed for people who were sick. They prayed for people who were grieving. And they covered prayer requests submitted by people in the congregation. But Oliver had never led the church to pray for evangelism. The prayer ministry team asked God to meet temporal needs, but so far as he knew they didn't pray regularly for the greatest eternal need—that the lost would come into a relationship with Jesus Christ.

That has to change.

Until recently, Oliver hadn't put much thought into the harvest fields Jesus mentions in Matthew 9:38, but now he knew that the first fields for Connection Church would be the community closest to the church. He and the other church members would have to become more actively involved in the surrounding neighborhood.

Sure, the members of the church knew people in the community. They knew many of the Rolesville merchants. Some of the families were involved in local sports leagues. But did the church really *know* the community as Jesus described it? Jesus not only knew who was in the fields, but he had compassion for them. His heart was broken for them.

Oliver wondered how the church could learn to love their community that deeply. They could look at the town's demographic data, but knowing a community from the heart is much more than numbers and profiles. They had to find ways to truly serve them, meet their needs, and reach them for Christ.

It was the *go* aspect of evangelism that Oliver found the most challenging. He didn't think his members would feel comfortable knocking on doors in the neighborhood unannounced. Indeed, many neighborhoods in Rolesville had a no solicitation policy.

"What does it mean to *go* into today's culture?" Oliver asked himself. "So many people seem to be resistant to anything having to do with religious faith."

Still, if he didn't lead and encourage the church to *go*, were they really being obedient to the Great Commission, which starts with the word *go*?

But Oliver wasn't discouraged. He knew if the people were obedient to God's commands that God would provide the path and the means. As he pondered this new direction, he was excited to see what God would do.

Oliver glanced at his phone and saw the time. He had been at the table alongside the trail for five hours. Time had flown. He checked his messages. Nothing urgent. Amazingly, no one had called.

As he walked the trail back to his car, he realized how much in his life he had to be thankful for. He knew several peers in pastoral ministry who were struggling and suffering greatly. He could not recall a time when there was so much angst and conflict in ministry. He'd had his share of challenges, of course, not the least of which was the recent kerfuffle with Ken. But God had been faithful throughout.

≡

Melanie was reading in the family room when he returned.

"Go get changed," she said as soon as he walked in. "We have reservations at Thomas's Steakhouse in forty-five minutes."

"What?" Oliver asked. "We just ate there a few weeks ago. I'm not sure we can afford another steak night so soon."

"Quit being such a fuddy-duddy," Melanie said. "We'll be fine. We're not going broke."

Oliver could not remember the last time he'd heard the word *fuddy-duddy*. He laughed and went upstairs for a quick shower and a change of clothes.

When they walked out to the garage, Melanie surprised Oliver by getting into the driver's seat.

"We need to get there on time," she said. "We can't have you driving like an old man through town."

"Okay, what's going on?" Oliver said as he went to the passenger side and climbed in. "I mean, I like it, but I'm confused."

"Let's get to Thomas's," Melanie replied as she backed the car out. "We'll have plenty of time to talk."

Oliver ordered the same as always: small filet, medium rare. Melanie surprised him by ordering a chicken entrée instead of her usual overdone filet.

Oliver could not hold back.

"Okay," he said emphatically. "Tell me what's going on. What have you done with my wife?"

Melanie smiled.

"We are celebrating your new position," she said.

Oliver looked at her quizzically.

"You're going to have a new church to pastor," she said teasingly. "It's called Connection Church, and it's located right here in Rolesville, North Carolina. From the outside, it might look the same as it ever was, but the church is developing a new heart and a new vision. You've been alone with God for the better part of the day, and you know he's calling you to lead this church in a new direction. And though there will undoubtedly be challenges and frustrations ahead, you are ready for it because God has prepared you for it."

Oliver was stunned. He couldn't have asked for a more specific and encouraging confirmation that he was on the right track than to have Melanie on board from the get-go. She was so perceptive, and she knew him so well. He marveled at her faith in God and always had.

"Well," she said, plucking a sourdough roll from the basket in the middle of the table, "the food will be here shortly. You might as well get started telling me everything about your day. I'm ready to listen. And by the way, congratulations on your new job."

8

SORTING IT ALL OUT

EVER SINCE THE REFERENDUM at the annual business meeting, there was a noticeable excitement in the church. The Vision Task Force members communicated freely with the congregation about their desire to offer a fresh vision for the church in the days ahead. The ordeal with Ken seemed to have caused people to become more open to change and more supportive of Oliver's leadership.

Oliver enjoyed the affirmation and the positive energy in the church, but he did not take it for granted. As a longtime pastor, he realized this was a bit of a honeymoon period and there would be more challenges ahead. As he had said on more than one occasion: "Everyone is for change until the change affects them personally."

Still, he was ready. The church was ready. God had prepared them for this moment.

The task force members sensed both the urgency and the opportunity. They scheduled a meeting for the following Thursday.

≡

On Thursday afternoon, knowing that the task force would need every minute available for discussion, Oliver stopped by his favorite local deli to pick up sandwiches and sides on his way to the church.

This way we can have supper while we talk.

He arrived in the church conference room at 4:30 and set out the food, along with bottles of water, pods for the coffee machine, and his own guilty pleasure: diet soda and chocolate chip cookies.

"They cancel each other out," he always told Melanie whenever she gave him a hard time.

At 4:45, Jorge arrived, followed by Becky, Emma, and Rob a few minutes later. Everyone seemed eager to get the meeting started.

"Please help yourselves to a sandwich and whatever else looks good," Oliver said as they gathered around the table. "I want to share with you some things God has been teaching me lately."

Oliver sensed that all eyes were on him, but it was Jorge who spoke first.

"Oliver, you look like a kid on Christmas Eve. I can't wait to hear what's new."

After blessing the food, Oliver took a sip of his diet soda and got down to business.

"As you all know, at our first task force meeting, we discovered that our average weekly attendance has declined by almost 20 percent over the past three to five years. As we looked for reasons, we identified three traps we've fallen into as a church, which I believe have undermined people's commitment to regular participation in the life of the church. Just to recap our findings before we move on to what I *really* want to talk about tonight, we found that (1) many members of the church do not believe the Bible, or they do not understand the basic truths of the Bible; (2) our church has a low bar of expectations of our members—we expect little and therefore we get little; and (3) our members do not understand or embrace the biblical meaning of church membership."

Emma, Becky, Rob, and Jorge nodded affirmatively as they ate their sandwiches.

"While I was on a little personal retreat one day last week, the Lord convicted me that perhaps the greatest trap we've fallen into is disobedience to the Great Commission. We have not consistently or meaningfully shared the gospel with our community. I'm also convinced that Satan has blinded us to this omission. The last thing he wants is more people following Christ."

"I think you're right on the money, Pastor," Rob said. "We can definitely do better."

"Here's the thing," Oliver continued. "We've been asking ourselves, 'Where have all the church members gone?' Well, one purpose for the church is to reach others with the good news of the gospel. But when churches don't evangelize, people don't see evangelism as essential to the life of the church. And if it's not important to bring *others* into the fold, it leads people to ask whether they need to be there themselves. It quickly boils down to a decision about whether to go to a church service on Sunday morning or do something else."

≡

Oliver took the next thirty minutes to explain his journey through the first part of the New Testament, and the connections he began to see during his time on the Neuse River Trail. He confessed that he had been blind to the biblical mandate for evangelism.

"In my view, this is our most glaring oversight, and the one most needing attention."

Jorge was typically not the first one to speak up at these meetings, but he was obviously moved by Oliver's heartfelt words.

"Isn't it amazing," he began, "when you discover something that was right in front of your eyes all along? I agree, Oliver, that this trap is perhaps our greatest failing. Do you have any thoughts about how to address this need?"

"I don't have all the specifics," Oliver responded. "But I'm convinced that local church evangelism must have three critical components. First, it must be preceded and accompanied by *prayer*. Jesus was clear that we must use the power of the Holy Spirit to reach people."

Oliver was pleased to see that everyone was fully engaged in the discussion and taking notes.

"Second," he said, "we must really get to *know* our community. We must focus on the harvest field that God has given us—and it begins on our doorstep. We particularly need to focus on those who live within fifteen minutes of the church. That *is* our community."

He paused for a moment to allow time for feedback. Everyone was nodding, but nobody spoke.

"Third," he said, "we must find ways to *go* into the community. Evangelism in the New Testament is clearly an active response of obedience. I'm not sure exactly what that will look like for us, but I know we need to go. I could summarize our action plan with these three key words: *pray*, *know*, and *go*."

"Wow," Becky interjected. "This mandate and your solution seem so obvious now. I don't know how we missed it."

"I think I know why we missed it," Emma said thoughtfully. "We've been so busy trying to do good things that we neglected the *greatest* thing—that is, the Great Commission."

Oliver noticed that Emma's comment seemed to hit Becky right between the eyes.

"Becky," he said with a smile. "It looks like you have an idea. Is there something you want to say?"

"Not right now," Becky responded. "But I have an idea I'd

like to bring up later. For now, though, let's continue with this conversation."

"Fair enough," Oliver replied. "We have a church that seems ready to move forward. God has dealt with some internal opposition we had. And we have been greatly blessed to be working together on this Vision Task Force. We have identified four hidden traps that have ensnared Connection Church. And now it's time to move from *dys*functioning to functioning. Would anyone like to suggest how we move forward?"

Emma spoke up first, bringing her business experience to bear on the situation.

"Well," she began, "we've identified at least four areas of suboptimal performance—*traps*, as we've called them. Though the church is not a business organization, we still must have processes in the church that address the challenges we face and allow us to be proactive toward our opportunities. In simple terms, if we want to move forward, our church members need to know what is expected of them and how they can do it."

Oliver loved how Emma always brought clarity to situations.

Rob immediately added his thoughts.

"Look," he said, "I know we're not going to get everything figured out in one meeting, but let's start by *outlining* an approach to each of the four traps. Can you tell I taught English before I became an administrator?"

Everyone laughed as he continued, "For example, the first trap is that many people do not understand biblical truths, or they don't believe them. Pastor Wagner has already added a deeper teaching element to his preaching, but what are some other practical steps we can take to deal with the issue of a lack of biblical belief and knowledge?"

"I've identified twelve key essentials of the Christian faith," Oliver replied. "And I plan to do a twelve-week sermon series on them. Then, each year after that, I will cover six of the essentials, which means my preaching will cover all twelve essentials every two years."

"That's great," Jorge commented. "I can also see that the problem of low expectations—which is another trap we've identified—overlaps with biblical unbelief. We must be very clear about what we believe. And our beliefs must be clear and explicit on our website. But we also need to include those expectations—*and* the biblical essentials—in a new members class."

Becky joined the discussion with enthusiasm. "If Oliver is going to preach through twelve essentials of the faith this year, and then cover six every other year, we can do the same thing in our community groups. I think community groups will become a major focus of the *new* Connection Church."

Oliver loved the energy in the room. Though the solutions that had been suggested were not a silver bullet, they were a great starting point. He was ready for the conversation to continue.

"Let's move on to the next two traps—dealing with low expectations and failing to embrace biblical church membership. We will obviously have to focus more specifically on each one, but as Rob has suggested, I want to at least touch on them all before we leave tonight."

"I like how you mentioned those two together, Pastor," Emma said, "because I see a close connection between them. I really think we can address them with a single solution for now."

"Go ahead, Emma," Oliver encouraged. "Let's hear your idea."

"Okay, one of the key reasons we have low expectations of church members is because we don't establish those expectations clearly on the front end."

"Exactly," Jorge chimed in. "A good new members class will set expectations and provide a framework for what it really means to be a church member biblically."

"Yes," Emma replied. "A class won't be the total solution, but it's a great starting point. I really think it can nip some of these other problems in the bud."

Oliver looked over at Becky, who was furiously taking notes. He could almost see the gears turning in her mind.

Emma turned to Oliver. "Since you've done the most thinking about this lately, Pastor, would you like to address the fourth issue—evangelism?"

"Absolutely. I'd like to continue to focus on the three areas I mentioned to you: *pray*, *know*, and *go*. For now, the first step is clear: I will ask the prayer team to start praying specifically for how we can reach non-Christians in our community. Those who are involved in the ministry are dedicated and committed to the power of prayer. I have no doubt they will be on board and excited to help."

Oliver paused to look through a stack of papers on the table in front of him.

"I have already ordered and received an incredible report on our community," he said. "It not only has tons of demographic data on everyone who lives within a fifteen-minute drive of the church, but it also has great information about their needs and their aspirations. But a report is only a start. We need to get outside our four walls and talk to people in the community. We need to hear from them directly."

"You know," Emma interjected, "most of our members know or work with non-Christians. We can encourage them to get to know these people better so we can be better equipped to share the love of Christ with them. Do you have any specific thoughts about the *go* part of obedience?"

"I'm still thinking that one through," Oliver responded. "But I have no doubt that we need to encourage our people to go into the community with intentionality, even if it's something as simple as prayer walking in a neighborhood. Our people need to be reminded again and again that 'the fields are *already* ripe for harvest.' Jesus himself says so in John 4:35. If we are obedient in the way we know best, I have no doubt that God will take care of the rest."

Though the task force seemed energized by the progress they had made, Oliver knew that the renewal of Connection Church would be a marathon, not a sprint. Even though it was earlier than he had planned to end the meeting, he thought it was a good place to stop. They had addressed each of the four major traps and had outlined a basic response. He was about to ask whether everyone was ready to call it a night when Becky spoke up.

"Before we leave tonight," she said, "can we address a potential *fifth* trap—one that I think could undermine our efforts to solve the other four? This was the idea you asked me about earlier, Oliver."

Seeing the others nodding in assent, Oliver said, "Okay, let's take a ten-minute break to stretch our legs and maybe get a cup of coffee, and then we'll dive back in."

≡

"I've been thinking . . . ," Becky began when the group had reassembled.

Oliver had to smile at her familiar intro.

"Up till now we've been addressing things we're *not* doing. We're not adequately teaching the essentials of the faith. We're not expecting enough of our members. We're not communicating the biblical meaning of church membership. And as Oliver noted tonight, we are not evangelizing.

"But here's the problem that *I* see: We don't have *time* to deal with these problems."

"Hold on, Becky," Jorge interjected. "What do you mean we don't have time? This is about *making* time for what's most important."

"That's all well and good," Becky responded, "but we're a *busy* church. Our calendar is full of activities. We don't have time to accomplish major objectives because we're so busy doing . . . *stuff*. We can't accomplish *great* things because we're too busy doing *good* things."

Becky got up and walked over to the whiteboard.

"Here's how I would articulate the fifth trap—and tell me what you think: Connection Church is too prone to be activity-driven, rather than focused on discipleship—that is, on helping members become (and grow as) committed followers of Jesus."

"I like it, Becky!" Rob said immediately. "We haven't really talked about this, but the idea of *discipleship*—helping people *become* followers of Jesus and *grow* as followers of Jesus—answers the other four traps as well. Discipleship has to be anchored in the truth of Scripture; and as people grow in their faith, they will want to be committed to the church—and to church membership—and they will want to reach out to others, as well."

"Well put, Rob," Jorge said. "So how do we begin to turn the ship in the direction we want it to go?"

"If I may," Emma interjected. "While the local church is definitely a spiritual outpost, it is also an organization. Putting my corporate management hat on, I agree wholeheartedly that we have many good ideas, but I can't imagine how we can implement them within our current structure. It's too complex, and as Becky said, we're all too busy."

"Well, I've been thinking," Becky said again. "The first thing we need to decide is what we can reasonably expect of our members in order for them to be functioning *disciples* in our church. We said that we must become a high-expectation church. So let me ask all of you: Going forward, what expectations will we have of every new member?"

She turned back to the whiteboard and wrote *Expectations* across the top.

"Okay, what are some basic expectations?"

Jorge spoke first. "We haven't said much about it, but I would hope that we would expect any member to be a *giving* member."

Becky wrote *giving* on the board.

Oliver liked where this process was going. "We want all members reaching the community with the gospel," he said.

Becky wrote *evangelism* on the board.

Emma was next. "I love the idea that we want to reach people who are not Christians, but we also want to make sure that the people in our church—members *and* nonmembers— understand the truth of the gospel."

"Hmm." Becky thought for a moment and then wrote *teaching/doctrine.* "I'm not sure that's the best way to say it," she added, "but we definitely want our new members to be committed to the truth of God's Word."

The room was quiet for a moment.

"Well, if we're talking about minimum expectations," Emma said, "I fully expect our members to attend worship services and get involved in a community group."

"Absolutely," Oliver said. "I don't know how we missed those two."

After another brief silence, Jorge said, "These expectations are a good starting point for us. But I want us all to leave tonight with some *structure* built around our ideas. It's one thing to identify our expectations. It's another thing to put them into practice at Connection Church."

"Good point," Oliver said.

"I think we're all in agreement that we will provide initial expectations to new members through a new entry-point class," Jorge continued. "When we do, we will address the second trap—our low-expectation culture—and also the third trap, that members do not understand the biblical meaning of church membership."

The others nodded in agreement, and Becky said, "I've been trying to think of a way to make this memorable, and I think I have an idea."

She turned back to the whiteboard and wrote *New Members Class*.

"So let's go back to the first trap," she said. "Many members of the church do not believe the Bible, or they don't understand the basic truths of the Bible. For clarity and brevity, how about if we boil that down to the word *believe*."

> **Trap #5**
>
> Churches are too prone to be activity-driven, rather than focused on discipleship—that is, on helping members become (and grow as) committed followers of Jesus.

She wrote *Believe* on the whiteboard before continuing.

"*Believe* implies that we will communicate the essentials of the Christian faith so that all members know them and affirm them."

Becky paused. Oliver could tell she had given this a lot of thought.

"Since we all agree that members should attend worship services faithfully and be active in a community group," Becky continued, "how about if we use the *belong* word again to capture that expectation."

"I like this," Jorge interjected, "and I have an idea for another one. But it doesn't start with a *b*. One of our expectations is that all members should be faithful financial givers to the church. So how about adding the word *give*?"

As Becky wrote *Give* on the whiteboard, Emma said, "Giving doesn't have to be just financial—though that's obviously important. But *give* also communicates the idea that we are to give generously of our *time*, as well, to serve others."

"Nice," Jorge said.

Then Rob spoke up. "We heard clearly from our pastor that our church must become an evangelistic church. So to balance the board with another *g* word, what if we captured that basic expectation with the word *go*."

"Wow, I see a four-point sermon taking shape there," Oliver said with a laugh.

Becky drew a line under each of the four points on the whiteboard and said, "In order to address the complexity and busyness of our church—which is the fifth trap—we need to focus our church activities on these minimal expectations."

- <u>Believe</u>
- <u>Belong</u>
- <u>Give</u>
- <u>Go</u>

"Amazing!" Emma exclaimed. "That brings such clarity to our priorities. We can begin focusing on these four areas, and over time we can eliminate or minimize other activities."

"It's almost as if our process of ministry or discipleship is also a vision statement," Jorge added. "Our vision as a church is to *believe, belong, give,* and *go.*"

Oliver was impressed. He had been the quietest one in the room, and the other members had led extremely well. He knew it was almost time to end the meeting, so he attempted to summarize where the church was, and where the church was going.

"You leaders are absolutely incredible," he said with a catch in his throat. "Just a few days ago, we were facing a major church conflict. We've also had to confront the harsh reality that Connection Church has fallen prey to five major traps. But we haven't focused on the negative; we've put our heads together and identified some great potential solutions."

Before continuing his thoughts, Oliver took a moment to make eye contact with each person at the table.

"I am nothing short of amazed at where we are today compared to where we began. I think we're already well on our way to developing a new members class with well-defined expectations and a clear understanding of biblical membership. We already have several things in motion so we can be clear about our beliefs, and so all new members will know and embrace them. We have plans to expect both evangelistic outreach and ministry within the church. And we will expect our members to be generous financial givers.

"I know we don't have the perfect blueprint, but we have an incredible beginning. And I know that we can expect challenges and opposition because we are earnestly seeking to do the work of God's Kingdom. We need to be prepared for some spiritual warfare."

Oliver was surprised to feel tears running down his face.

"But I also know that the battle is ours to win. There is no challenge, no opposition, and no problem we cannot overcome in God's power. I hereby declare tonight that Connection Church is not merely a renewed church, but we are a *new* church, newly committed to God's mission on earth."

Oliver saw that there were tears in the eyes of the other leaders as well.

"Let's end this meeting tonight with a new dedication. Let's give this church to God, perhaps like we've never done before. Let's pray to that end."

With those words, Oliver surprised himself by getting down on his knees to pray.

The other leaders joined him on their knees as well.

Connection Church was truly becoming a new church.

9

WHERE DOES YOUR CHURCH GO FROM HERE?

THE STORY OF CONNECTION CHURCH likely rings true of your own church in some ways. Indeed, at Church Answers, our team has worked with thousands of churches with similar characteristics. I wouldn't be surprised if you saw a lot of parallels between your church and this fictionalized story.

For Oliver and Connection Church, it began with an unsettled feeling and took a major turn with an innocuous question about a church member named Jill, who most of the leaders were unaware had not attended the church for some time. That discovery led to a reality check, some soul-searching, conflict, and resolution.

As we saw, churches today are confronted with declining attendance, both from the departure of members and attenders and from a drop in the attendance frequency of members. Here's a reminder of how many attenders a typical church loses in a year.

TYPICAL WORSHIP ATTENDERS LOST IN A YEAR PER 100 IN ATTENDANCE	
Attendance frequency decline	15
Moving out of the community	9
Transfer to another church	7
Death	1
Total	32

Of course, every church is different, but these numbers are at least indicative of the challenge that churches face. Simply stated, a typical church must replace 32 percent—almost one-third!—of its attenders every year just to stay even. In a church of fifty, that's sixteen people. In a church of 400, it's 128!

Perhaps the most challenging statistic is the declining attendance frequency of some members. If every member of a one-hundred-member church attended every week (I know, highly unlikely!), the average attendance would obviously be one hundred. But if all those members decided to attend every other week, the average attendance would drop to fifty. In other words, without losing a member for any other reason, that church's weekly attendance would decline by 50 percent.

Of course, the story of Connection Church is more than a story of numbers. I hope you sensed the hearts of these fictional characters. A healthy church is first a church with spiritually healthy church members. Connection Church was doing little to foster the growth of its members. Therefore, the losses should not have been unexpected.

Making the Connection to Your Own Church

When we left the Connection Church task force meeting, they were moving toward a general plan, but without many specific ministries and actions. That was intentional. Because every church is unique, we do not have a one-size-fits-all solution. But in this concluding chapter, we will offer some resources and some possible solutions for your church.

Furthermore, we have gathered a variety of resources and solutions at WhereHaveAllTheChurchMembersGone.com, and we are constantly updating the website with new ideas. When you see an asterisk (*) in this chapter, it indicates that we have a possible tool for your church to use to address that particular issue.

Now let's look at some next steps Connection Church might have taken after their final Vision Task Force meeting. Our hope is to inspire a level of creativity for your church to discover its own God-given solutions.

Reality Check/Soul-Searching

I cannot overstate the importance of this initial step. Many church leaders and members refuse to look at the current state of their church. And because they are often oblivious to the challenges, they don't address them.

A simple step of discovery is to look at your church's current average worship attendance for the past five years. Keep it simple. With any luck, you'll have a single number for each year. You will see trends both good and bad. Though this step is only a start, it's an important start. Oliver didn't like counting "nickels and noses," so he didn't make it a priority to track attendance or giving. Fortunately, Becky *did* make it a priority. Her recordkeeping identified a problem that most of the leaders and members were unaware of.

Your church cannot move toward greater health if you are unwilling to evaluate where it might be sick today.

Like some of the leaders at Connection Church, your church can interview some of its members—very active, less active, inactive, and maybe some who have moved on. The leaders at Connection Church sat down with a few members who represented different perspectives in the church.

Another option is to conduct a formal survey of your church members.* I encourage you to find a survey that has been tested and used for several years.

It is critical for your church to know the composition and demographics of your local community. You can get basic data from the US Census Bureau, or you can get a report specifically designed for churches to use.* You can't *reach* your community unless you *know* your community.

These points of discovery are just to get you started. Go to WhereHaveAllTheChurchMembersGone.com for more. Your church will never even get to the point of creating God-given solutions until you take the time to go through a discovery process. You can do it on your own, or you can call an outside consultant to help.* Regardless of your path, you must clearly understand your church's current reality.

Conflict

This is the messy stage of the process. After you've discovered the state of your church's health in the reality check/soul-searching stage, you will undoubtedly begin to experience some level of conflict. It only makes sense. Your discovery will lead to a desire for solutions—and that means change. And change inevitably leads to conflict.

Please hear me clearly. Conflict is normal, and if handled well it can lead to positive solutions. Unfortunately, many leaders are not prepared for conflict. They can feel like failures, as if their leadership is causing division in the church.

I encourage church leaders to at the very least understand the basics of change and conflict management. There are countless resources* and studies available. Conflict is as old as creation, and it is a normal, and probably necessary, part of church life. There will be no good resolutions without conflict.

Resolution

First, let me remind you of the five key traps that silently kill churches.

1. Too many people in the church either do not believe the Bible or do not understand the basic truths of the Bible, because the church is not teaching the foundational truths of Scripture.
2. Churches have a low bar of expectations for their members, and they have not clearly articulated whatever expectations they have.
3. Church members (and nonmembers) do not understand or embrace the biblical meaning of church membership.
4. Churches fail to obey Christ's command to reach non-Christians with the gospel.
5. Churches are too prone to be activity-driven, rather than focused on discipleship—that is, on helping members become (and grow as) committed followers of Jesus.

All five of these traps are common in many churches. It is rare that a church has none of them. The first trap—biblical illiteracy and biblical unbelief—has become increasingly common. It is not unusual for a church that identifies as conservative and Bible-believing to have a plurality of members—and sometimes a majority of its members—deny such basic doctrines as the exclusivity of salvation through Christ (see John 14:6).

It is particularly heartbreaking to see the reactions of pastors and key church leaders when they discover their congregation is ensnared in this trap. Often they can't understand how their church got to this point. Other the other hand, they soon have to admit that they have done little to communicate and reinforce the essentials of the Christian faith.

The path that Connection Church took to address this problem is instructive. They decided to clearly communicate core beliefs in their new members class. Their pastor became much more intentional about clearly communicating the essentials of the faith through his preaching. And the leadership committed to utilize the church's small groups to reinforce the basics of the Christian faith on a recurring basis.

A number of resources* are available for use in these groups and in other settings. But do not assume that your members understand and agree with the church's core beliefs. We recommend some type of congregational survey* to discover what your members really believe.

The second trap is having low expectations. Unfortunately, most churches are low-expectation churches. They know their members are busy in other areas of their lives, and they don't want to ask too much. So they ask too little. Disarming this trap requires a change in culture to move toward becoming a high-expectation church. Though cultural change often depends on pastoral leadership, the tone of high expectations can be set in a new members class. If you don't establish your expectations right up front, you run the risk of creating a "bait and switch" scenario down the road.

The third trap is failing to help church members understand the biblical meaning of church membership. This trap overlaps with the second one. If your members truly understand what the Bible teaches about church membership, they will have little trouble thriving in a high-expectation church culture.

Sadly, the fourth trap is pervasive in North American churches. It seems as if many, if not most, church leaders and members have evangelistic amnesia. They seem oblivious to the clear mandate given by Jesus and supported throughout the New Testament to share the gospel and make disciples.

The fifth trap is busyness—which is also a trap in the wider culture. Most churches are not prepared for solutions because they're too busy doing activities without a clear purpose. Becoming a simpler church might serve your church well.

A Proposed Model

To be absolutely clear, there is no one-size-fits-all model for churches. Context means everything. Leaders are different. Members are different. And God has a unique plan for every congregation. Keep that in mind as you consider the following model.

First, ask yourself a basic question: At a minimum, what should you expect all your church members to do? You will begin the journey toward high expectations by deciding prayerfully what the basic expectations should be. Again, these are *minimum* expectations; they are not limitations on other ways that church members can carry out Christ's mission.

In the case of Connection Church, they articulated the following minimum expectations:

- Every new member must go through a new members class* where information about the church is given and expectations are established.
- Every new member must learn and affirm the essential beliefs of the Christian faith.* These beliefs will be taught in the new members class and reinforced through the community groups and preaching ministry.
- Every member is expected to faithfully attend worship services regularly (that is to say *often*) and to be an active member of a community group.*

- Every member is expected to give of their time to be involved in at least one ministry* in the church each year.
- Every member is expected to give generously* of their financial resources to the church.
- Every member is expected to be involved in some type of evangelistic ministry* in the community at least once a year.

Again, these are foundational expectations, not limiting expectations. We can summarize these expectations in four easy-to-remember words:

Believe
Belong
Give
Go

These expectations should be introduced and reinforced through a new members class.

Believe
- Members will learn the essentials of the Christian faith, beginning in the new members class and continuing in community groups and in the preaching ministry.

Belong
- Members will faithfully attend worship services.

- Members will be active in community groups.

Give
- Members will give of their time to be involved in at least one ministry in the church each year.
- Members will share their financial resources by faithfully and regularly giving to the ministry of Connection Church.

Go
- Members will be involved in at least one evangelistic ministry per year, where the gospel message is shared in the community.

As this simple outline begins to characterize your discipleship process, you may find that it also serves as an effective vision statement for the church: Believe. Belong. Give. Go.

If you're familiar with my other books, you may have noticed that this process was first communicated in *Simple Church*, which I wrote with Eric Geiger. Though *Simple Church* was first published in 2011, its principles are still relevant and useful today.

It's not unusual for churches to have the most difficulty getting their church members to *go*—to get involved in sharing the gospel of Christ in the community. We have discovered some effective ways that churches are addressing this challenge. Be sure to look for the most current resources at WhereHaveAllTheChurchMembersGone.com.

A Case for Optimism

It is common to be concerned about the current state of churches in our nation and beyond. On the one hand, that's healthy. It means we are confronting reality. On the other hand, the avalanche of negative news can be dispiriting and discouraging.

I remain an obnoxious optimist about our churches. The primary reason for my positive attitude is my unrelenting belief in the love of God the Father, in the work of Christ the Son, and in the power of the Holy Spirit in our churches.

A second reason for my optimism is that we are already seeing many churches become healthier. They are reaching people with the gospel, ministering in Christ's name to the community, and growing as fruit-bearing disciples of Christ. At Church Answers, we work with such churches every day. And we see how God is working in these churches.

Where should you and your church begin? Ultimately, that is a question that only you and your members can answer. It depends on your desire to hear from God in your own specific context. Through the story of Connection Church, you may have seen some significant gaps in your own church's ministries. If so, filling those gaps could very well be your starting point.

Many churches may need a fresh start. While I am not suggesting that you close your doors, clean house, and reopen, you might need to ask God to guide you through a major overhaul of your church. If that's the case, you can use our suggested model as a starting point. As you pray and discuss and pray some more, God will give you clarity about how to adjust it and contextualize your process as you commit yourselves to doing his work with greater fervency.

Here are some basic questions to get you started:

- Do we have a well-planned and implemented new members class? Do we need to start fresh with a new model?* New members classes go by different names in different churches. Don't get hung up on terminology. Just make sure you have something that accomplishes the purpose of supplying information and establishing expectations.
- Does our new members class begin with the gospel? Anyone who is not a Christian must understand how to become a follower of Christ.
- Have we made clear the minimum expectations of all members in the new members class?
- Do we have clearly stated places of ministry in our church so that members can meet the basic expectations?
- Does our church focus on discipleship and minimize or cut nonessential activities? In other words, is our church a simple church or a complex church?*
- Do we have a clear plan to get our members involved in evangelism?* That is typically a big hurdle for churches to overcome.

What about Your Existing Members?

The model I offered focuses on changing a church's culture by establishing high expectations for new members. It does not specifically address existing members. In the story of Connection Church, the leadership decided to "grandfather" their existing members. In other words, existing members did not have to go through the new members class or agree to minimal levels of service and commitment. Such an exception is not ideal, but it may be necessary to get things rolling. In churches we have worked with that move by forward focusing on new members, we often see existing members increase their own levels of commitment.

Although it isn't necessary in our model to establish a vision statement (or a formal process of discipleship) such as *Believe, Belong, Give, Go*, we have found that it helps tremendously to keep the vision and expectations visible in the church. A number of pastors we know preach on each aspect of the vision statement every year.

Though we recommend that churches minimize or cut nonessential ministries and activities—that is, ministries and activities that don't directly support the renewed direction of the church—we urge you to be careful and wise. Eliminating "sacred cow" ministries can become controversial and distracting to the greater mission of the church. You will often need prayerful patience to remove complexity and busyness from your church.

Where Have All the Church Members Gone?

The story of Connection Church is a common one in our experience. Some members leave churches because they aren't Christians. They are what theologians call "unregenerate members" because they never truly became followers of Christ. You can't be committed to Christ's church if you are not committed to Christ himself.

Other members leave because they don't see the importance of church involvement. They view it as just another optional activity. So if travel sports, for example, become important to them, they will substitute that activity for church attendance.

The most common way that church members leave the church is not by abdicating their membership, but by attending less often. This form of "quiet quitting" has become epidemic in North American congregations. It is a clear sign that churches have low expectations of their members. Members who view the church as just another organization don't grasp the biblical reality that the local church is the primary focus of the New Testament from Acts 2 to Revelation 3. As I've said many times before—and others have as well—the local church is God's plan A for his mission on earth, and he did not give us a plan B.

Many churches are in decline because they have chosen to disobey and disregard the Great Commission. Evangelism is the glaring deficiency of more than 90 percent of the churches we've studied.

Still, I remain an optimist. I wish you could see the churches we work with every week. I wish you could see how some of them are transforming from unhealthy to healthy. Though not great in number, they are clear indicators that God is not done with our local churches.

I offer the same encouragement to you. God is not done with your church. God is not done with your ministry. Through him all things are possible, including the turnaround and renewed health of unhealthy churches.

Where have all the church members gone?

My prayer for you and your church is that you will soon replace that question with an exclamation of praise: "Look at all the people God is bringing to our church!"